Paper Tigers:
China's Nuclear Posture

Jeffrey Lewis

Paper Tigers:
China's Nuclear Posture

Jeffrey Lewis

IISS The International Institute for Strategic Studies

The International Institute for Strategic Studies

Arundel House | 13–15 Arundel Street | Temple Place | London | WC2R 3DX | UK

First published November 2014 by **Routledge**
4 Park Square, Milton Park, Abingdon, Oxon, OX14 4RN

for **The International Institute for Strategic Studies**
Arundel House, 13–15 Arundel Street, Temple Place, London, WC2R 3DX, UK
www.iiss.org

Simultaneously published in the USA and Canada by **Routledge**
270 Madison Ave., New York, NY 10016

Routledge is an imprint of Taylor & Francis, an Informa Business

© 2014 The International Institute for Strategic Studies

DIRECTOR-GENERAL AND CHIEF EXECUTIVE Dr John Chipman
EDITOR Dr Nicholas Redman
COPY EDITOR Jemimah Steinfeld
EDITORIAL Jill Lally, Anna Ashton
COVER/PRODUCTION John Buck, Kelly Verity

The International Institute for Strategic Studies is an independent centre for research, information and debate on the problems of conflict, however caused, that have, or potentially have, an important military content. The Council and Staff of the Institute are international and its membership is drawn from almost 100 countries. The Institute is independent and it alone decides what activities to conduct. It owes no allegiance to any government, any group of governments or any political or other organisation. The IISS stresses rigorous research with a forward-looking policy orientation and places particular emphasis on bringing new perspectives to the strategic debate.

The Institute's publications are designed to meet the needs of a wider audience than its own membership and are available on subscription, by mail order and in good book-shops. Further details at www.iiss.org.

Printed and bound in Great Britain by Bell & Bain Ltd, Thornliebank, Glasgow

British Library Cataloguing in Publication Data
A catalogue record for this book is available from the British Library

Library of Congress Cataloging in Publication Data

ADELPHI series
ISSN 1944-5571

ADELPHI 446
ISBN 978-1-138-90714-0

Contents

ACKNOWLEDGEMENTS

Writing a book is an exercise in humility. The process of creating and revising a manuscript is not possible without the support and guidance of friends and colleagues.

I am especially indebted to Mark Fitzpatrick at the International Institute for Strategic Studies who suggested that I revisit the topic of China's nuclear forces, policy and posture for an *Adelphi* book. Writing an Adelphi had long been a career goal, I am grateful to Mark for making it possible and helping me along the way. Nick Redman at IISS is a superb editor, as well as a subject matter expert in his own right. Working with IISS was a pleasure.

The Monterey Institute of International Studies, where I teach a class on China's nuclear weapons program, has been an exceptionally supportive home thanks to the efforts of Dr. William C. Potter, the Director of the James Martin Center for Nonproliferation Studies. While writing and teaching, I had the opportunity to work with a number of talented graduate students who will, in time, no doubt make their own contributions on the subject of China's nuclear weapons. I am very grateful to Catherine Dill, Pan Fangdi and Jonathan Ray for lending a hand with research, translation and insight.

Several colleagues were generous enough to look at one or more draft chapters. The text would be far more flawed if not for the help of Henry Boyd, Scott Carson, Michael Chase, Gregory Kulacki, Joshua Pollack and Mark Stokes. Their comments save me a great number of blushes. Any remaining errors of fact or interpretation remain mine alone.

Finally, I am thankful to my wife, Jill, and our children for their support and forbearance while I struggled with the manuscript.

A2AD	anti-access/area denial
AEDS	Atomic Energy Detection System
AIT	American Institute in Taiwan
ATACMS	Army Tactical Missile System
CANDU	CANada Deuterium Uranium
CAS	China Academy of Sciences
CCP	Chinese Communist Party
CCTV	China Central Television
CMC	Central Military Commission
CNNC	China National Nuclear Corporation
COSTIND	Commission of Science, Technology and Industry for National Defense
CPGS	Conventional Prompt Global Strike
CSIS	Center for Strategic and International Studies
CTBT	Comprehensive Nuclear-Test-Ban Treaty
CTBTO	Comprehensive Nuclear-Test-Ban Treaty Organization
ERW	enhanced radiation warhead
FMCT	Fissile Material Cut-off Treaty
GWe	gigawatt electrical
HEU	highly enriched uranium
ICBM	intercontinental ballistic missile
ICF	inertial confinement fusion
IHE	insensitive high explosives
IMS	International Monitoring System
INET	Institute of Nuclear and New Energy Technology

IRBM	intermediate-range ballistic missile
ISAB	International Security Advisory Board
LEU	low-enriched uranium
LTBT	Limited Test Ban Treaty
MAD	mutual assured destruction
Mb	body-wave magnitude
MW	megawatt
MOX	mixed oxide fuel
MRBM	medium-range ballistic missile
MTCR	Missile Technology Control Regime
NASIC	National Air and Space Intelligence Center
NEM	Nuclear-explosive materials
PLA	People's Liberation Army
PLAN	People's Liberation Army Navy
PUREX	Plutonium Uranium Extraction Plant
PRC	People's Republic of China
RV	reentry vehicle
SAR	synthetic aperture radar
Second Artillery	The strategic missiles forces of the PLA.
SLBM	submarine-launched ballistic missile
SRBM	short-range ballistic missile
SSBN	ballistic missile submarine
Sub-kiloton weapon	Weapon with a yield equivalent to less than 1,000 tonnes of TNT.
SWU	separative work unit. A measure of work expended in the enrichment process, used to quantify centrifuge output.
TEL	transporter-erector launcher
TTBT	Threshold Test Ban Treaty

China's nuclear arsenal has long been an enigma for Western policymakers and issue experts. The arsenal has historically been small, based almost exclusively on land-based ballistic missiles, maintained at a low level of alert, and married to a no-first-use doctrine – all choices that would seem to invite attack in a crisis. Chinese leaders, when they have spoken about nuclear weapons, have articulated ideas that sound odd to the Western ear. Mao Zedong's oft-quoted remark that 'nuclear weapons are a paper tiger' seems to be bluster or madness.

Western officials and experts often express frustration at the level of transparency and dialogue with the Chinese government and other interlocutors. Given China's growing economic, political and military influence, its small nuclear force looms ever larger in Western calculations. Our collective inability to understand the logic behind China's nuclear forces, policy and posture is frustrating.

In an earlier work, I argued that the Chinese arsenal was not so strange if one accepted the notion that China's leaders simply viewed nuclear weapons differently to their Western counterparts – or acted as though they did.[1] For a variety of bureaucratic, historical and ideological reasons, Chinese leaders have placed less emphasis on technical details than their Western counterparts when it comes to assessing the stability of deterrence.[2] Imagine Chinese political leaders left cold by the econometric logic of Albert Wohlstetter's *Delicate Balance of Terror*, just as we Westerners find little to recommend in Mao's earthy aphorisms.

China's nuclear forces are now too important to remain a mystery. Yet Westerners continue to disagree about basic factual information concerning one of the world's most important nuclear-weapons states. Chinese statements are often cryptic or simply difficult for foreigners to accept. Meetings among Westerners and Chinese seem to cover the same ground, year after year. Enlightenment is elusive.

These disagreements replicate themselves in fundamental ones about how, as a policy matter, the United States and its allies should approach China's nuclear forces. In the US, this debate takes the form of a question about 'whether China is a small Russia to be deterred or a large North Korea to be defended against'.[3] The implicit distinction in this phrasing is whether Washington accepts that China's nuclear forces provide an inescapable measure of deterrence as Russia's do, or whether some combination of nuclear and conventional weapons including missile defences could allow the US to prevail in a conflict where China used its nuclear weapons.

In one sense this is an artificial debate. The notion that the US would accept Russia or the Soviet Union as an equal never commanded formal consensus in the US – the descriptor mutual assured destruction (MAD) was a calumny. In another sense, it has the comfort of the familiar; Washington did accept the notion of mutual deterrence with Moscow implicitly. Recent statements from the Obama administration suggest that, whatever reluctance may inhibit a public recognition of mutual deterrence with China, the administration treats China and Russia as like cases, distinct from North Korea.

This *Adelphi* book documents and explains the evolution of China's nuclear forces in terms of historical, bureaucratic and ideological factors. It argues that China's nuclear force, policy and posture look the way they do because of circumstance. There is a strategic logic, but that logic is mediated through politics, bureaucracy and ideology. The simplest explanation is that Chinese leaders, taken as a whole, have tended to place relatively little emphasis on the sort of technical details that dominated US discussions regarding the stability of deterrence. Such a general statement, however, smoothes over the debates and divisions that make the evolution of China's deterrent so interesting.

This book is also, at least implicitly, a critical reading of US intelligence estimates regarding China's nuclear weapons and missile programmes. Although a considerable amount of open-source information is now available regarding the history of China's strategic weapons programmes, this has only recently been the case. For many years, Western analysts had to rely on declassified or leaked intelligence assessments that often turned out to be wrong or incomplete. The overall record of US intelligence analyses of Chinese capabilities was excellent in hindsight, but analysts struggled to understand decisions in terms of Chinese politics, often substituting a sort of post hoc explanation burdened with American assumptions and attitudes. What China was doing was often more clear than why it was doing it.

Questions about the kinds of arguments the Chinese have among themselves, both about Chinese society in general and about the nature of nuclear weapons, illuminate the limits of imagining China as a 'little Russia' or a 'big North Korea'. If we are to think in this vein, perhaps China is an 'inscrutable

France'! Such an answer may seem silly, but so is the notion that China is best understood as a Russia, a North Korea or any country other than itself. Just as a zen *koan* creates a brief, liberating moment of rupture that illuminates a question, laughing at a nonsensical answer to a nonsensical question can allow a reader to abandon confining analogies and develop an understanding of the Chinese nuclear arsenal on its own terms.[4] What that understanding might be for China's nuclear forces, policy and posture is argued in the following pages.

Notes

[1] Jeffrey Lewis, *Minimum Means of Reprisal: China's Search for Security in the Nuclear Age* (Cambridge, MA: MIT Press, 2007). For a more recent review, see: Jeffrey Lewis, 'China's Nuclear Modernization: Surprise, Restraint, and Uncertainty', in Ashley Tellis, Abraham Denmark and Travis Tanner (eds), *Strategic Asia 2013–2014: Asia in the Second Nuclear Age* (National Bureau of Asian Research, 2014), pp. 67–98.

[2] These factors are discussed in more detail in Jeffrey Lewis, 'Chinese Nuclear Posture and Force Modernization', *Nonproliferation Review*, vol. 16, no. 2, July 2009, pp. 197–209.

[3] William Perry, Brent Scowcroft and Charles Ferguson, *U.S. Nuclear Weapons Policy*, Independent Task Force Report No. 62 (New York, NY: Council on Foreign Relations, 2009), p. 45.

[4] The phrase brief 'liberating moment of rupture' is borrowed from Frithjof Schuon, 'Remarks on the Enigma of the Koan', *Studies in Comparative Religion*, vol. 5, no. 2, Spring 1971.

CHAPTER ONE

Chinese views of nuclear weapons

Studies of Chinese attitudes towards nuclear weapons can be built on quotations from various leaders, starting with Mao himself, but collections of Maoist aphorisms can also be orphaned from time and context. World leaders have a distressing tendency to say one thing about nuclear weapons while doing another. US president Dwight D. Eisenhower, for example, once expressed dismay at the notion of 1,000 or more nuclear-armed 0 (ICBM), yet he bequeathed his successor a programme to build 1,950 *Minuteman* missiles. This chapter documents changes in how Chinese leaders have viewed nuclear weapons. It attempts to show the evolution of Chinese views about nuclear weapons as reflected in actual policy. The remarks of Mao and other leaders are an essential part of this discussion, but only when presented in their proper context.

The best-recalled of Mao's quotations was the assertion, repeated in propaganda frequently during his lifetime, that nuclear weapons were a 'paper tiger' – a claim that usually strikes Western observers as peculiar, especially for the leader of a nuclear-armed state. The statement, however, is consistent with larger Maoist themes about the triumph of socialism over better-armed imperialists and politics over superiority in arms.

From the earliest stages of China's efforts to acquire nuclear weapons, Chinese leaders thought of the nuclear-weapons programme in terms of the overall level of China's industrial and technological development rather than specific military requirements. The origins of China's programmes to develop thermonuclear weapons and ballistic missiles lie in the same period of technological and industrial ambition that produced China's Great Leap Forward (1958–61).

An emphasis on mastery of technologies accounts for the ambitious goals set for the nuclear-weapons programme – an immediate emphasis on thermonuclear weapons and ICBMs starting from the late 1950s. China's mid-1960s ambition to beat France in testing a thermonuclear weapon reflects the same mindset that produced the Great Leap Forward era's emphasis on surpassing the UK in steel production. Yet while its leaders were eager to hurdle to the front ranks of technology, China was slow to deploy operational nuclear forces in the interim, which reinforced a tendency to neglect the details of nuclear strategy and operational plans. In a November 1968 discussion with E.F. Hill, an Australian communist, Mao said, 'Our country, in a sense, is still a non-nuclear power. With this little nuclear weaponry, we cannot be counted as a nuclear country. If we are to fight a war, we must use conventional weapons.'[1]

Then there were China's turbulent domestic politics. The command-and-control of nuclear weapons was a sensitive political issue, intertwined with China's leadership politics, which centred, in part, on control of the armed forces. One can see general trends in Chinese thinking about nuclear weapons, particularly a pervasive belief that nuclear weapons are primarily instruments of political coercion, as well as the related view that small numbers of weapons would suffice to neutralise larger arsenals used in this manner. However, China would not develop a formal nuclear strategy and operational plans until after Mao's death in 1976 and the deployment of the first ICBMs in the early 1980s.

Today, China's forces and policies continue to develop largely along the trajectory set in the mid-1980s under Deng Xiaoping's leadership, even though the country has changed markedly. Technology has also changed dramatically in the intervening decades, particularly with the emergence of precision conventional-strike forces – the 'Revolution in Military Affairs' widely recognised to have taken place after the Gulf War (1990–91). China's leaders are now facing increasingly effective missile-defence and precision-strike capabilities. Although China's policy of nuclear no-first-use is likely to remain in place, these new conventional capabilities pose a serious challenge to how Chinese leaders approach nuclear weapons.

The Korean War and after

Chinese state media dates China's decision to pursue nuclear weapons to January 1955. This date falls after the Korean War (1950–53) and during the 1954–55 armed conflict over a series of islands between China and Taiwan now known as the First Taiwan Strait Crisis. The date also corresponds to the Soviet Union's public announcement of the intention to aid China in developing a peaceful nuclear energy programme. At that time, Chinese premier Zhou Enlai addressed a plenary meeting of the Chinese State Council, confirming that the Soviet announcement was the result of recent negotiations and offering the first rationale for the Chinese nuclear-weapons programme.[2]

Revisiting Zhou's speech challenges the simple narrative that 'nuclear blackmail' drove China to acquire nuclear weapons. Chinese and American sources both emphasise the role of US nuclear threats in prompting Chinese interest in nuclear weapons. Many Americans believe that US nuclear threats compelled Beijing to accept Washington's armistice terms in Korea in 1953. Chinese state propaganda asserts that US nuclear threats related to the dispute over Taiwan's status compelled China to seek nuclear weapons of its own.

On balance, archival evidence does not support either view. Chen Jian notes the lack of evidence in Chinese archives linking US nuclear threats to the evolution of Beijing's attitude toward the armistice.[3] Indeed, there is little evidence that any nuclear threat was conveyed to Beijing.[4] Chinese leaders accurately assessed the capabilities and limitations of the US nuclear stockpile, as well as the political constraints on the US use of nuclear weapons. China's leaders concluded that nuclear weapons might be useful for political coercion, but did not offer decisive military capabilities. Such a view is broadly consistent with their ideologically determined beliefs about the importance of fighting a 'people's war'.

Similarly, Chinese interest in nuclear weapons preceded the First Taiwan Strait Crisis, which began in August 1954. One does not need to explain Chinese interest in nuclear weapons during this period; it would have been surprising only if China had decided to forgo such capabilities. At that time, there was no norm against nuclear weapons. The presumption was that if a state could build nuclear weapons, it would.

China began negotiating with Moscow in October 1954 for nuclear assistance, culminating in the January 1955 announcement when Zhou addressed the Chinese State Council. In his speech, Zhou made a series of arguments about why China sought nuclear weapons. Although Zhou emphasised the role of US nuclear coercion, he made a counterintuitive point that was a recurring theme in Chinese propaganda of the period: the US engaged in nuclear coercion because its policymakers

1958 Guidelines for Developing Nuclear Weapons

1. Our country is developing nuclear weapons in order to warn our enemies against making war on us, not in order to use nuclear weapons to attack them. This is conducive to the support of the international proletarian revolutionary movement and colonial independence movement.

2. The main reasons for us to develop nuclear weapons are to defend peace, save mankind from a nuclear holocaust, and reach agreement on nuclear disarmament and the complete abolition of nuclear weapons.

3. To this end, we have to concentrate our energies on developing nuclear and thermonuclear warheads with high yields and long-range delivery vehicles. For the time being we have no intention of developing tactical nuclear weapons.

4. In the process of developing nuclear weapons, we should not imitate other countries. Instead, our objective should be to take steps to 'catch up with advanced world levels' and to 'proceed on all phases [of the nuclear programme] simultaneously'.

5. In order to achieve success rapidly in developing nuclear weapons, we must concentrate human, material and financial resources. We have to concentrate superior forces to fight a war of annihilation. Any other projects for our country's reconstruction will have to take second place to the development of nuclear weapons.

6. It is time for science and scientists to serve the Party's policies, not for the Party's policy to serve science and scientists. Therefore, we must guarantee the Party's absolute leadership of this [nuclear-weapons] project. We need to strictly adhere to the politics, to strengthen the political and ideological education of staff and patriotic education.

7. We have to train a new team of nuclear scientists and technicians in the shortest time, who are from worker and peasant families. As long as we have manpower, we will be able to generate development in various undertakings. The task of training successors [for the nuclear-weapons programme] is as important as the manufacture of nuclear weapons.

8. We must set up a separate security system so as to guarantee absolute secrecy.

Initial translation by Xue Litai. Supplemental translation by Pan Fangdi were, in fact, far more terrified by the prospect of a nuclear war than their Chinese counterparts. Zhou asserted that Chinese leaders did not regard nuclear weapons as 'special' in the sense of having a unique power to compel – that was an American notion. What China would do, Zhou argued, was 'master' nuclear technology, to replace any sense of terror with scientific understanding. This understanding of nuclear weapons, combined with what Chinese leaders regarded as a correct ideological outlook, would eliminate China's vulnerability to American coercion. The US would be far too frightened by the reality of a Chinese bomb to continue engaging in the sort of coercion that Chinese leaders believed they were being subjected to in the Taiwan Strait.

This view is evident in the 'Guidelines for Developing Nuclear Weapons', probably drafted by the Central Military Commission, in June 1958.[5] The guidelines start by making clear that the purpose of China's nuclear weapons would be to 'warn' its enemies against war, not to attack them. To that end, the guidelines establish thermonuclear weapons and ICBMs – what would later be described as 'sophisticated weapons' – as the preferred forces, explicitly eschewing tactical nuclear weapons. The guidelines repeat the theme of Zhou's 1955 speech, warning China not to 'imitate' other powers presumably frightened by nuclear weapons, but to catch up and keep pace with their technological achievements – the goal of mastery that would place China on equal footing with other major powers and immunise it against nuclear coercion.

Paper tigers

Zhou's arguments are broadly consistent with the Maoist emphasis on the importance of ideological considerations over sheer material factors in the outcome of any struggle. As early as 1946, Mao had declared that reactionaries and atomic bombs were 'paper tigers' – things that appear frightening, but have no power. Referring to enemies or their weapons as paper tigers alludes to an earlier concept of 'the superiority of men and politics' over weaponry, an important consideration for a People's Liberation Army (PLA) that could expect to continue facing enemies equipped with superior arsenals, including nuclear weapons. The notion itself is derived from a Leninist maxim about the ideological commitment of cadres being more decisive than modern weapons in war. [6]

A trove of documents, usually referred to as the 1961 'Secret Chinese military papers', helps to illustrate the role that ideological statements played in creating guidance for military leaders and their units. Sometime in late 1961 or 1962, the US intelligence community acquired the 1 January–26 August 1961 issues of a secret PLA military newsletter, *Bulletin of Activities*, distributed to officers at the regimental level or above. The *Bulletin* includes important speeches and ideological guidance for military leaders. These constituted the major source of evidence for early US assessments about Chinese views of nuclear weapons and nuclear warfare. The State Department released the trove to the National Archives in 1963, allowing scholars to translate and analyse the contents.[7]

Strategic thinking in China about nuclear weapons would remain limited to this broad ideological commitment to master the same technologies as other major powers. 'Peking has not yet produced a full-fledged doctrine on nuclear warfare and may not do so until after an effective nuclear capability has been developed, and perhaps not until Mao Tse-tung has passed from the scene', the late Ralph Powell, a professor of Far Eastern Studies at American University who was stationed in China from 1941–48, anticipated in 1968. 'Mao's preconceived ideas have had somewhat the same retarding effect on atomic doctrine, but not on the development of nuclear weapons, that Stalin's "permanently operating factors" had in the Soviet Union.'[8] Events in 1969 would demonstrate Powell's prescience.

No-first-use

China's pledge to not under any circumstance be the first to use nuclear weapons has evolved into the single best-known element of China's nuclear-weapons policy. It became a staple of Chinese diplomacy with the release of a statement announcing China's first nuclear test in 1964. Until the mid-1950s, Beijing had tended to support Soviet diplomatic policies, particularly Moscow's arms-control proposals. The idea of a no-first-use pledge had appeared in appeals for disarmament, as well as in diplomatic propaganda, alongside the broader effort to ban the use of nuclear weapons. Popular appeals, such as the 1950 Stockholm Appeal promoted by French physicist Frederic Joliot Curie, mentioned a prohibition on the first use of nuclear weapons. The Soviets made a similar proposal in 1955. But the Chinese, before October 1964, showed no special interest in no-first-use.

After hints of growing independence from the Soviet line in Chinese foreign policy during the late 1950s, Moscow and Beijing broke over Soviet support for negotiations leading to the Limited Test Ban Treaty (LTBT). A ban on atmospheric tests would have imposed a significant constraint on China's nuclear arsenal. To add insult to injury, the Soviets justified suspending their aid to China's nuclear programme in a June 1959 letter warning that continued assistance might jeopardise test-ban talks with the US. The Chinese, in response, would denounce the LTBT upon its signing in 1963 as 'a big fraud to fool the people of the world'.[9]

During the 1959–64 period, China developed a number of arms-control proposals to deflect pressure applied by other developing countries that supported efforts to ban atmospheric nuclear testing.[10] Zhou Enlai visited ten African countries in December 1963 and January 1964, where, according to Morton Halperin and Dwight Perkins, at the time scholars at Harvard University, he 'was sharply questioned about China's unwillingness to sign the Test Ban Treaty, not only by newsmen in press conferences but also by government officials…'[11] Zhou used China's support for nuclear-weapons-free zones, especially an African one, and a proposal for a summit of world leaders to discuss the 'complete prohibition' of nuclear weapons, to blunt criticism of China's opposition to the test ban. Zhou found support among African nations for a regional nuclear-weapons-free zone, but little interest in his summit proposal.

After China's first nuclear explosion in October 1964, Beijing dropped proposals for an Asian nuclear-weapons-free zone in favour of Zhou's notion of a summit of world leaders to discuss the prohibition of nuclear weapons. Modern reproductions of the October 1964 statement announcing China's first nuclear explosion are usually abridged, often omitting the summit proposal. China envisioned a no-first-use pledge as the central obligation of the nuclear-weapons states that might emerge from such a meeting. In addition to the formal statement announcing the first nuclear test, Zhou sent a cable to other heads of state that was far more measured in tone, proposing such a summit.[12]

No-first-use arose from a specific diplomatic need to reduce pressure on China to join the ban on atmospheric nuclear explosions, a step that would have stunted the development of its nuclear-weapons capabilities. China's no-first-use policy also embodied Zhou's notion that threats to use nuclear weapons in fact reflect a debilitating fear of such weapons. The full statement of October 1964 contains several paragraphs on ideological considerations relating to nuclear weapons, explaining Mao's paper tiger notion, expressing fealty to Marxism–Leninism and reaffirming that the outcome of a war is decided by the people, not any weapon.[13] No-first-use appears at the end of a Maoist sermon on the nature of human history, war and nuclear weapons.

The pledge is, therefore, less a promise to others than the obvious policy arising from Beijing's view that Washington engaged in nuclear coercion because nuclear weapons were what US policymakers feared most. Threats by China to use its nuclear weapons against weaker states would undermine Chinese claims that the numerically superior US nuclear force had little coercive value. For those inclined to regard no-first-use as a false promise, it's clear that Mao did not intend the statement to be reassuring to Washington or Moscow. The tone of the official communiqué is aggressive, hectoring and a little self-righteous.

Almost immediately, China demanded that the US issue its own no-first-use pledge. Beijing viewed the demand as a test of whether or not the US would continue to subject China to what it described as 'nuclear blackmail'. In addition to Zhou's diplomatic cable proposing a disarmament summit, China also relayed a proposal for a bilateral no-first-use pledge to the US through a channel in Warsaw. The US rejected the proposal. When, some months later, the United States deployed a *Polaris* missile submarine to Asia, the Chinese response in the weekly Peking Review established no-first-use as a test of US intentions:

> Shortly after its first nuclear test, China proposed to the United States that the Governments of both countries should issue a formal statement pledging that neither of them would at any time or under any circumstances use nuclear weapons. If the United

States had any sincere desire for peace, it would have been easy to reach an agreement…[14]

With the 1964 statement, China had in place the ideological and policy components of its early thinking about nuclear weapons. Nuclear doctrine and operational concepts would have to wait for China to deploy credible forces and, more significantly, for Mao to die.

Politics of command-and-control

Over the course of the 1960s, China pursued the development of thermonuclear weapons and an ICBM. China tested a staged thermonuclear weapon in 1967 and conducted a partial-range test of a DF-5 ICBM in 1971.[15]

China's technical progress, however, was not matched by the deployment of significant nuclear forces (see Chapter Four), a formal nuclear strategy or even operational concepts relating to command-and-control. Chinese thinking remained highly ideological during this period, a tendency reinforced by the growing chaos of the Cultural Revolution, a mass movement inspired by Mao that tore apart the Chinese leadership beginning in May 1966.[16]

The nature of the political struggle among factions, including for control of the armed forces, prevented any effort to develop a plausible nuclear strategy or operational concepts for the nuclear forces that China was developing.

Recent scholarship has focused on the role of China's nuclear forces during the 1969 crisis with the Soviet Union, particularly whether China's nuclear forces were placed on alert during this period and what this might tell us about Chinese thinking. Sino-Soviet relations deteriorated steadily throughout the 1960s and war appeared possible following border skirmishes that started when Chinese forces fired on a Soviet patrol on the disputed Zhenbao (Damansky) Island in the Ussuri River in March 1969.

The resulting 1969 Sino-Soviet crisis is an important episode in Chinese foreign policy. It grew out of Chinese wariness following the violent Soviet suppression, in August 1968, of the Prague Spring movement in Czechoslovakia, as well as the growing turmoil of the Cultural Revolution. Mao, whose leadership of the Chinese Communist Party (CCP) replaced that of a Soviet faction in the 1930s, remained wary of Soviet ambitions – and more than willing to paint his opponents as agents of Moscow. It was during this period that Mao apparently returned to the notion of improving relations with the US, which he described as the 'far away enemy' in contrast to nearer foes such as the Soviet Union, India and Japan. The Sino-Soviet crisis was the immediate cause of a well-known report – signed by four eminent Chinese leaders who had attained the rank of Marshal, including Nie Rongzhen – that proposed improving relations with the US as a counterbalance to Soviet influence.

The crisis, which began with skirmishing in the spring before descending into a nuclear crisis in the autumn, is the first instance of ground-combat between two nuclear-armed states. It resulted in both an implicit Soviet nuclear threat against China and an unusual episode in which China's nuclear forces are sometimes said to have been placed on alert. The entire episode, however, is so intertwined with the politics of the time that even today an objective understanding is difficult to reach. The so-called alert of 1969 demonstrates how difficult it can be to understand nuclear weapons decisions outside of their immediate political context.

Available information about this crisis largely comes from Zhang Yunsheng, who was aide to Lin Biao – Mao's heir apparent in 1969.[17] The crisis seems to have deepened following what some believed to be a Soviet threat to use nuclear weapons in an unofficial radio broadcast. Zhang claims Chinese leaders became increasingly concerned about the possibility of a Soviet attack in October 1969.

As tension grew, the Chinese government undertook a number of war preparations. In mid-October, the Central Committee ordered China's leadership to disperse along the Beijing–Guangzhou rail line: Mao went to Wuhan; Lin Biao went to Suzhou; Zhou Enlai remained behind in Beijing as a crisis manager, as did Lin's ally General Huang Yongsheng, the head of the army.

The reason for the dispersal, as well as the actual level of concern, remains disputed. Some accounts describe the attitude within the Chinese leadership as 'panic'. Yet Mao's physician, Li Zhishui, described Mao as calm during his stay in Wuhan.[18] Other leaders who were evacuated – such as Nie Rongzhen – argue that Lin pushed for the evacuation to isolate his political rivals.[19] Lin, who died in an air crash in 1971 after allegedly plotting a coup, did use the October 1969 evacuation of Beijing to place the Second Artillery's first commander, Xiang Shouzhi, under house arrest in the countryside.[20] It is unclear, however, whether the ultimate force behind the evacuation was Lin or, in fact, Mao himself.

Once the evacuations occurred, the dispersed leadership communicated by telephone, setting the stage for China's first experience with the command-and-control of strategic forces. Once in Suzhou, Lin continued issuing guidance for implementing the Central Committee's decision on war preparations.[21] Lin verbally dictated six general points to his aide Zhang Yusheng. One of the six points stated that China's nascent missile forces must be ready to launch at any time. The aide wrote down the points, then discussed them with Lin's wife, Ye Qun, who suggested they clarify that Lin was not ordering an immediate launch. Having written down Lin's six points, the aide then telephoned General Huang in Beijing. Huang, in turn, telephoned a subordinate, tasking him with rendering Lin's broad guidance into an actionable military order. The subordinate reformatted the six points in the form of a series of four directives to different institutions, issued under the authority of Lin as the Vice Chairman of the Central Military Commission. 'Directive No. 1' resulted in a massive redeployment of Chinese ground forces. 'Directive No. 2', which has not been declassified, transmitted Lin's guidance that the Second Artillery must be ready to launch at any time. General Yan tried to get General Huang's approval to issue the six principles in the form of four directives, but Huang was not available. As a result, General Yan issued the order in Lin's name without further approval. Ye Qun, Lin's wife, called Mao's bodyguard, Wang Dongxin, to inform Mao about the order. Mao and others would later claim that Lin acted alone to usurp Mao's authority although this is far from clear.[22]

Chinese accounts do not explain what precise order was given to the Second Artillery. Lin himself seems to have been improvising, given that Zhang suggested Lin further clarify he was not ordering units to fire the missiles. Since China has not declassified Directive No. 2, we can only guess how Huang and his staff interpreted Lin's guidance.

One suggestion is that the alert meant arming any deployed missiles with warheads, then erecting – but not fueling – them.[23] But what if, as Mao implied to E.F. Hill, China had deployed no ballistic missiles in late 1969? US intelligence assessments did not detect DF-2 deployments until the early 1970s, although they may have missed small, camouflaged deployments.[24] If China had no deployed ballistic missiles, Directive No. 2 may have been meant for units at China's missile-test sites where DF-2 and possibly DF-3 testing was being conducted. This would explain a puzzle. In one account Lin seems to have ordered DF-3s to be placed on alert, even though China had no such missiles at the time. Lin misunderstood defence-industry reports on the development of the missile. In another account Huang's staff made provision for the launch of test missiles in extreme circumstances. At the time, China had modified some aircraft to conduct nuclear tests. Chinese sources suggest Chinese leaders would have considered these assets for operational missions in extreme circumstances, such as the October 1969 crisis.

The crisis lacks a clear end. China's leaders trickled back into to Beijing, although the factionalism continued. Mao was apparently displeased at the notion of an order in the name of the vice chairman – Lin Biao – that seemed to usurp his own authority. The standard Chinese interpretation of this event is that Lin's orders were a dress rehearsal for the failed 1971 coup that resulted in Lin's attempt to flee to the Soviet Union and the ensuing fatal plane crash in Mongolia. A lively debate exists about the accuracy of the official Chinese account of Lin's actions, but Mao used the event to purge the uniformed ranks of General Huang and other senior officers close to Lin. Lin's alleged treachery remained a live issue in Chinese politics for years afterward, with Lin's supporters tried in 1981 as part of a broader series of trials against the Gang of Four (four prominent CCP officials) and their supposed allies.

The nature of the charges against Lin illustrates the challenge of building a nuclear strategy or developing operational practices in Mao's China. China had no formal command-and-control structure. The act of issuing orders to military units was highly political. Some contemporary declassified US intelligence assessments noted the lack of strategic or operational writings regarding nuclear weapons during Mao's lifetime. The reticence of military officers to raise issues relating to nuclear policy is easy to understand given the politics associated with Lin's Directive No. 2. It was not until after Mao's death in 1976 and Deng Xiaoping's subsequent consolidation of power that discussion of nuclear policy began in earnest. Xiang Shouzhi, who returned from tending pigs to lead the Second Artillery a second time in the mid-1970s, only to be sent away again, was offered a third stint as commander of the Second Artillery. He declined, making clear he preferred pigs to his colleagues in Beijing.

What little evidence exists for discussions on nuclear weapons in the 1970s relates to basing locations and modes, and whether China's new ballistic missiles would be deployed in silos, caves or some other mode. Attention to operational considerations fell short of detailed planning that might be integrated with China's nuclear policy or strategy.

Developing operational concepts

After Mao's death, Deng Xiaoping consolidated his authority, eventually pushing aside Mao's chosen successor Hua Guofeng. Deng's leadership involved a return to more rational policy planning, as well as an ideological assessment that the international environment was, for the time being, essentially peaceful, allowing China to pursue economic development rather than prepare for war and revolution.

At the same time, China began deploying small numbers of DF-4 and DF-5 ICBMs. The leaders of the Second Artillery began to think about developing formal operational concepts for the country's nuclear forces, hosting symposia and establishing a research committee that would develop materials on nuclear strategy and operational practices. This process resulted in the production of a series of texts, including The Science of Second Artillery Campaigns, one of the main sources that foreign analysts have relied upon when seeking to understand the development of China's nuclear strategy and operational plans.

The Second Artillery convened a pair of symposia in December 1979 and July 1981, which resulted in new work regulations, alongside a military glossary. In 1983, they established an academic department at the Academy of Military Sciences, China's top military research institute, followed by a committee for academic research to formulate a 'science of operations' and 'operational principles and rules' for missile units.

The committee concluded that China required a formal nuclear strategy to translate broad policy guidance relating to no-first-use and overall military strategy into plausible operational concepts for deployed nuclear forces.[25] The committee sought permission to draft a comprehensive nuclear strategy that, following a series of meetings in 1987, was approved by the Central Military Commission in 1989.

Texts such as *The Science of Second Artillery Campaigns* dominate US discourse about Chinese thinking on nuclear weapons in the same way that the *Bulletin of Activities* did in the 1960s. The new nuclear strategy, according to Lewis and Xue, represented 'a meaningful break from the past' by articulating a notion of a 'self defensive strategy' that would import the language of deterrence into the role of nuclear weapons in China's security.[26]

Other commentators see more continuity with the past, although some Chinese officials and experts have become more comfortable with the term 'deterrence', which initially only applied to the US and was treated as a synonym for coercion. The term usually associated with deterrence in Mandarin is '*weishe*', which carries a connotation of coercion not present in English and usually describes how foreign powers, especially the US, use nuclear weapons.[27] The point may seem an abstract one, but it can lead to confusion since some Chinese speakers use the term '*weishe*' to mean coercion exclusively in the context of foreign nuclear strategy, while others use it as English speakers might, either to facilitate dialogue or as a result of an English-language education.

There is an ongoing debate in Western circles about whether China's no-first-use policy represents a real operational constraint on the Second Artillery.[28] This debate arises from Chinese military writings and other materials that point out the problems of a categorical pledge to never be the first to use nuclear weapons under any circumstances. The practical difficulties associated with such a pledge are, of course, well documented in the strategic literature of Western countries, where policymakers and strategists have long rejected such a policy as destabilising and, in the colourful acronym favoured by certain bureaucracies, NOFUN (no-first-use of nuclear weapons).

In the Chinese context, conversely, 'no-first use' is better understood as an ideological statement about the nature of nuclear weapons. These considerations touch on the legitimacy and authority of specific leaders, as well as the party in general.

Another interpretation of the debates about no-first-use, then, is that the discussions represent a continuing effort to develop plausible operational concepts for China's nuclear forces within the strictures of policy. Nuclear strategy, in China, links policy imposed from above with operational requirements developed by the military. Nuclear strategy can help mediate the tension between the requirements for operationally credible forces and the political imperative of no-first-use.

While to all appearances there are Chinese military and policy experts who would prefer some other policy to no-first-use, the Second Artillery seems to have focused on debates about how to implement the policy rather than a frontal assault on the policy itself. The rise of conventionally armed missiles in the Second Artillery, married to a fundamentally different set of operational concepts, suggests that the Second Artillery's interests increasingly lie in conventional capabilities. It is unclear whether the interest in conventionally-armed missiles results from disdain for no-first-use or the limitations of nuclear weapons in general.

The challenge of creating plausible operational concepts for China's nuclear forces under no-first-use arises from the growing ability of conventional weapons to hold at-risk strategic targets. For example, in 2010, Japan's *Kyodo News* acquired a copy of *The Science of Second Artillery Campaigns* and reported that the document contained plans to abandon no-first-use in the face of attacks on nuclear power plants, dams and other civilian targets.[29]

The text, however, makes a more complex point. China might consider a shift in its declaratory posture – what Beijing will say about nuclear weapons – to prevent an impending attack with conventional weapons that would produce mass civilian casualties.[30] In early 2000, some Taiwanese and US strategists began openly discussing the use of conventional weapons against urban populations or high-value targets such as the Three Gorges Dam. Conventional strikes that cause mass casualties are particularly difficult to deter under the strictures of no-first-use. Reportedly, Chinese planners chose to reserve the right, subject to the decision of the political leadership, to announce a change in their declaratory policy in the unlikely scenario that the US or another country threatened to use conventional weapons to disarm the country's nuclear forces or drown millions of Chinese citizens by destroying a dam. This position on deterring conventional attacks with nuclear weapons is somewhat similar to the current US position on using nuclear weapons to deter biological-weapons attacks. That is, the US offers a clean assurance that it will not use nuclear weapons to respond to biological-weapons attacks, while reserving the right to change the policy in response if states should develop biological weapons truly capable of mass casualties.[31]

Contemporary Chinese thinking

China's development of plausible operational concepts and a formal nuclear strategy arose in connection with its deployment of silo-based, liquid-fueled ICBMs in the early 1980s. The deployment of solid-fueled, road-mobile ICBMs, and soon also submarine-launched ballistic missiles, creates an incentive to arm some missiles with warheads. China, too, is changing rapidly. The military is vastly more professional and the political leadership, on the whole, remains committed to suppressing the sort of factionalism and turmoil that defined Mao's China. A major policy question is whether the manner in which Chinese decision-makers have historically treated nuclear weapons will offer a reliable guide to their future actions.

The 1990s were a difficult time for Sino-American relations, culminating in the so-called great debates of 1999 in China. Following the international opprobrium resulting from the suppression of the Tiananmen Square protests in June 1989, the US–China relationship suffered through a series of crises relating to Taiwan's democratisation, allegations of espionage and non-proliferation issues. The NATO-led intervention in Kosovo and accidental US bombing of the Chinese embassy in Belgrade prompted an examination of the Deng-era consensus that the prevailing international trend was toward peace and development.[32] China's defence budget grew, as did investment in new capabilities, such as lasers and hit-to-kill systems that could be used in anti-satellite and missile-defence roles.[33]

Throughout this period, China sought to persuade the US to adopt no-first-use. These efforts were unsuccessful, although the two sides agreed to mutual 'non-targeting' in 1996. This effort was probably driven by growing Chinese concern about the effect of future US missile-defence deployments on the credibility of Chinese deterrent, which rested on a small number of DF-5 ICBMs. Those deployments were relatively recent; while China had deployed a pair of operational silos in the early 1980s, deployment of all 18 DF-5s was not complete until the early 1990s. Just as China was potentially deploying a credible deterrent, the US embarked on a programme of strategic modernisation, including missile defences, which by virtue of its size appeared to threaten China's small deterrent.

As noted in the preceding section, Chinese experts and officials have long treated a bilateral no-first-use pledge as a rough proxy for whether the US accepts that China has a credible deterrent and so cannot be subject to US nuclear coercion. China's diplomatic efforts to seek this pledge are roughly analogous to internal US debates about whether it should accept so-called mutual vulnerability with China.

Despite occasional expressions of concern among Western analysts, no-first-use – as an ideological assertion about the nature of nuclear weapons – appears likely to remain the defining feature of Chinese nuclear-weapons policy. This likelihood may be obscured by a Western tendency to seize on statements by Chinese officials that call into question China's commitment to it. These doubts are, in large part, motivated by a sincere belief among many Western analysts that any such pledge lacks credibility.[34] So, for example, when a Chinese expert, Chu Shulong, admitted that China might abandon the policy in extreme circumstances, the Office of the Secretary of Defense highlighted this as evidence of growing doubts about no-first-use.[35]

Most recently, a Chinese Defence White Paper omitted any reference to no-first-use, leading to concerns that China might be on the verge of dropping, modifying or otherwise making ambiguous the pledge.[36] An early response from a well-known Chinese military academic was somewhat equivocal, reiterating the principle but also implying that US policies might force a reassessment. Subsequent official statements have been more direct. General Qi Jianguo, the Deputy Chief of the General Staff of the PLA, used a speech at the 2013 Shangri-La Dialogue in Singapore to gently chide those who made such a 'close study' of Chinese texts. 'I want to solemnly declare that the Chinese government will never abandon the policy of no first use of nuclear weapons, which has been maintained for half a century. It has been proven in reality that it not only meets the national benefits of China, but also benefits the survival of all human beings.'[37]

Under the circumstances, those in China who would change China's policy of no-first-use are as unlikely to succeed as those who would wish to see Washington adopt a no-first use policy. The Second Artillery's shift toward conventional missiles, with a much more offensively oriented doctrine, would seem to indicate a relative decline in the position of nuclear weapons in Chinese security policy, rather than a prelude to the embrace of a different doctrine. This trend probably reflects a continuing view among Chinese leaders that nuclear weapons are intended for political coercion. In this sense, the Chinese view appears to represent historical continuity.[38]

There remain real questions about how China would reinforce deterrence should it appear to falter or even begin to fail. The most recent Defense White Paper, alongside some Chinese texts, makes clear that China plans on using alert levels to signal resolve. 'If China comes under a nuclear threat', the 2013 paper states, 'the nuclear missile force will act upon the orders of the [Central Military Commission], go into a higher level of readiness, and get ready for a nuclear counterattack to deter the enemy from using nuclear weapons against China.'[39] Similar concepts are found in the chapter on Second Artillery operations in *The Science of Campaigns* and *The Science of Second Artillery Campaigns*.[40]

As will be discussed in Chapter Four, China appears to store warheads separately from missiles in peacetime, while keeping its first generation of ballistic missiles unfuelled and its solid-fuelled, road-mobile missiles in garrison.[41] In a crisis, these units would disperse, either to hardened locations where they could ride out an attack or to other camouflaged locations. China has an extensive network of underground facilities to allow Second Artillery units to ride out an attack.[42] Chinese leaders appear to believe that such measures will enhance the survivability of the Chinese nuclear forces, as well as convey the will to retaliate against a nuclear attack.

Chinese materials also touch on the communications strategy that would accompany a decision to increase the alert status of the Second Artillery, noting the importance of using radio, television and the Internet to publicise the step of placing China's nuclear forces on alert. As noted in the preceding section, the Second Artillery might propose altering the no-first-use policy in conjunction with these steps if Chinese leaders believed that an adversary planned to use conventional weapons to create mass casualties or to negate China's nuclear forces.

A major issue today for Chinese attitudes regarding nuclear weapons is the growing possibility that US conventional weapons could hold China's nuclear forces at risk. Although most serious US analysts do not believe conventional weapons will substitute for nuclear ones in missions relating to destroying enemy nuclear forces, at least not in the foreseeable future, Chinese observers are increasingly alarmed by the potential of highly precise conventional forces to deny China its deterrent, perhaps in conjunction with missile-defence deployments. 'Chinese officials and analysts working on nuclear deterrence issues have expressed deep worries about the effect that CPGS (Conventional Prompt Global Strike) could have on the survivability of China's nuclear arsenal', as James Acton has noted. 'In fact, Chinese concerns about the effect of advanced conventional capabilities on the nuclear balance may be more acute than more documented concerns about ballistic missile defense.'[43]

Whereas Chinese policymakers have treated nuclear weapons as essentially unusable, suitable only for coercion, the possession of precise conventional weapons appears to place fewer constraints on China's adversaries. If no-first-use is an ideological statement about the inherently limited role for nuclear weapons, it poses questions about how to deal with conventional weapons that might have strategic effects. Although China appears to emphasise defence measures to enhance the survivability of its nuclear forces, the matter does not seem settled among Chinese strategists, and has emerged as a neuralgic issue in Chinese-American dialogues.

The growing Chinese concern about CPGS and other capabilities suggests that Beijing is anxious about how increasingly accurate conventional weapons may shape the international security environment.[44] China itself is investing heavily in conventionally armed short-, medium- and intermediate-range ballistic missiles (MRBMs and IRBMs) and cruise missiles, as well as anti-satellite weapons that would allow Beijing additional options to deal with US military capabilities. Beijing is also developing so-called boost-glide systems to enhance its growing conventional-strike capabilities.

Such capabilities, however, more deeply entangle US and Chinese conventional and nuclear forces, creating new and potentially unexpected risks. China's anti-satellite programmes, which may in part reflect a desire to counteract

US missile-defence efforts, have become an important rationale for the US conventional-strike capabilities that alarm Beijing. Ultimately, the possibility that Beijing might disable US satellites that provide missile warning, reconnaissance, navigation or communications might make escalation to nuclear use more likely, not less.

Neither Washington nor Beijing has fully thought through the implications of these new technologies, nor do the parties have a sufficiently developed strategic dialogue that allows them to begin addressing potential sources of strategic instability. These challenges are explored more fully in Chapter Five.

Conclusion

The evolution of China's thinking about nuclear weapons roughly mirrors the country's transition from the Maoist era of ideological certainty and technical inferiority to its present, market-oriented authoritarianism. Chinese leaders initially viewed the task of the country's strategic weapons programmes as one of mastery – mastering the same technologies as other major powers. Strategic considerations during this period were largely limited to Maoist conceptions of the role of nuclear weapons, further constrained by the vicious leadership politics that distorted policy planning, slowed the pace of deployments and interfered with the establishment of command-and-control arrangements. During this period, the various ideological conceptions underpinning China's limited deterrent that were initially expressed in the notion of the atom bomb as a paper tiger came to be imbued in the policy of no-first-use. Chinese leaders have consistently seen nuclear weapons as, fundamentally, tools of political coercion rather than useful battlefield instruments.

Following Mao's death, Deng Xiaoping consolidated power, opening an era of reform that curtailed the worst excesses of the Mao years. China during this period began deployments of nuclear forces such as the DF-4 and DF-5, and the Second Artillery began a process of developing plausible operational concepts for it nuclear forces.

Much of what appears to be a debate within China over no-first-use is probably better understood as part of this process of developing plausible operational concepts for the Second Artillery's nuclear forces within the strictures of an enshrined ideological statement about the role of nuclear weapons. No-first-use is a long-term component of nuclear strategy and imposes real challenges for Chinese planners as the security environment changes. It's particularly complicated by the now looming prospect of US conventional-strike capabilities, which raise questions relating to strategic stability that neither country has yet to fully grasp.

Notes

[1] Chen Jian and David L. Wilson (eds), 'All Under the Heaven is Great Chaos: Beijing, the Sino-Soviet Border Clashes, and the Turn Toward Sino-American Rapprochement, 1968–1969', Cold War International History Project, Bulletin 11, 1998: p. 159, http://www.wilsoncenter.org/sites/default/files/CWIHPBulletin11_p3.pdf.

[2] Address by Zhou Enlai at the Plenary Session of the Fourth Meeting of the State Council, 31 January 1955, http://digitalarchive.wilsoncenter.org/document/114333.

[3] Chen Jian, Mao's China and the Cold War (Chapel Hill, NC: University of North Carolina Press, 2001), pp. 85-117.

[4] The Eisenhower administration decided in May 1953, in principle, to consider the use of nuclear weapons if armistice negotiations broke down. There is no credible evidence that the decision was conveyed to the Chinese. Secretary of State John Foster Dulles later claimed to have conveyed a threat through Indian prime minister Jawaharlal Nehru, but Nehru denied this and declassified accounts of the meeting support Nehru.

[5] Guo Hualun, Study of Mao Zedong's Military Thinking: Essays on Military Issues of the Communist Bandits (Republic of China: Unknown imprint, 1 January 1973). A partial translation appeared in John Wilson Lewis and Xue Litai, China Builds the Bomb (Stanford, CA: Stanford University Press, 1988), p. 70. A full translation is available in this volume.

6   Ralph L. Powell, 'Great Powers and Atomic Bombs Are "Paper Tigers"', *China Quarterly*, vol. 23, 1965, pp. 55–63.

7   J. Chester Cheng, Ch'inglien Han, Gene T. Hsiao and Yin-tso Hsiung (eds), *The Politics of the Chinese Red Army: A Translation of the Bulletin of Activities of the People's Liberation Army* (Stanford, CA: Stanford University, 1966). For a historical perspective on the importance of these documents, see Eugene W. Wu, 'Library Resources for Contemporary China Studies', in David Shambaugh (ed.), *American Studies of Contemporary China* (Armonk, NY: M.E. Sharpe, 1997), p. 266. For analysis of these documents, see John W. Lewis, 'China's Secret Military Papers: Continuities and Revelations', pp. 68-78 and Alice Langley Hsieh, 'China's Secret Military Papers: Military Doctrines and Strategy', pp. 79-99, both in *China Quarterly*, vol. 18, April–June 1964. See also J. Chester Cheng, 'Problems of Chinese Military Leadership as Seen in the Secret Military Papers', *Asian Survey*, June 1964, pp. 864–72.

8   Powell, 'Great Powers and Atomic Bombs Are "Paper Tigers".

9   'Statement of the Chinese Government Advocating the Complete, Thorough, Total and Resolute Prohibition and Destruction of Nuclear Weapons Proposing a Conference of the Government Heads of All Countries of the World', 31 July, 1963, published in *Peking Review*, vol. 6, no. 31, 2 August 1963, pp. 7–8.

10 China was sensitive to the political costs of atmospheric testing. Initial Chinese plans called for the fourth nuclear test to be conducted underground, despite the results of early underground tests being unsatisfactory. China later conducted many nuclear tests using aircraft in order to reduce the resulting fallout, both radioactive and political.

11 Morton Halperin, *Communist China and arms control* (Santa Barbara, CA: Praeger, 1965).

12 Zhou Enlai, 'Cable to All Heads of Government Proposing a World Summit Conference on the Prohibition and Destruction of All Nuclear Weapons', *Peking Review*, vol. 8, no. 43, 23 October 1964, p. 6.

13 'Statement of the Government of the People's Republic of China', 16 October 1964, available in *Peking Review*, vol. 7, no. 42, 16 October 1964, pp. ii–iv.

14 Chinese government statement, 'Protest Against U.S. War Provocation', *Peking Review*, vol. 8, no. 1, 1 January 1965, p. 20.

15 China's nuclear testing programme is described in Chapter Two. The development of China's ballistic-missile programme is described in Chapter Three.

16 The Cultural Revolution in China lasted until the death of Mao and the arrest of the so-called 'Gang of Four' in October 1976.

17 In addition to Zhang's account (Zhang Yunsheng, 'Discussing Lin Biao's "Number 1 Order",' (in Chinese) *China News Digest*, 14 January 2003, http://www.cnd.org/HXWZ/ZK03/zk323.gb.html, other accounts are Mei Xinsheng and Gao Xiaoling, *Memories of Lin Biao's Secretary*, (China Federation of

Literacy and Art Circles Publishing Corporation, 1988), pp. 316–24; Tu Men and Xiao Sike, *Super Trial,* (Jinan, 1992) pp. 204–09; and Chi Zehou 'In Biao and the "Number 1 Order" Revisited,' *China News Digest*, 11 February 2003, http://www.cnd.org/HXWZ/ZK03/zk327.gb.html.

18 Li Zhishui, *The Private Life of Chairman Mao* (London: Chatto & Windus, 1994), pp. 504–19.

19 Nie returned to Beijing in February 1970, ostensibly for medical treatment. He managed to meet Mao, who urged him to stay in Beijing, and submitted his formal request to do so through Zhou, thus cutting out Lin.

20 John Lewis and Xue Litai, *Imagined Enemies: China Prepares for Uncertain War* (Stanford, CA: Stanford University Press, 2006), p. 175. See also: Frederick C. Teiwes and Warren Sun, *The Tragedy of Lin Biao: Riding the Tiger During the Cultural Revolution* (London, Hurst, 1996).

21 *Ibid.*, pp. 61–62.

22 *Ibid.*, p. 64.

23 This is what Saudi Arabia did when it alerted its DF-3 missiles in response to Iraqi missile attacks in 1991. See Khaled bin Sultan, *Desert Warrior: Personal View of the Gulf War by the Joint Forces Commander* (New York: Harper Perrenial, 1996).

24 Communist China's Weapons Program for Strategic Attack, NIE 13-8-71. Available at: http://www.foia.cia.gov/sites/default/files/document_conversions/89801/DOC_0001098170.pdf.

25 John Lewis and Xue Litai, 'Making China's Nuclear War Plan', *Bulletin of Atomic Scientists*, vol. 68, no. 5,

September 2012, pp. 45–65. This article is based on a longer Chinese article by Lewis and Xue.

26 *Ibid.*, p. 48.

27 *Weishe* is often used for concepts of both deterrence and compellence.

28 For a description of recent debates, see Michael S. Chase, 'China's Transition to a More Credible Nuclear Deterrent: Implications and Challenges for the United States', *Asia Policy*, vol. 16, July 2013, pp. 85–88, http://www.nbr.org/publications/asia_policy/free/ap16/Asia_Policy_16_July2013.pdf; and Taylor Fravel and Evan Medeiros, 'China's Search for Assured Retaliation', *International Security*, vol. 35, no. 2, Fall 2010, pp. 78–80.

29 'China military eyes preemptive nuclear attack in event of crisis', *Kyodo News*, 5 January 2011.

30 For a discussion of these passages, see Gregory Kulacki, 'Chickens Talking With Ducks: The U.S.-Chinese Nuclear Dialogue', *Arms Control Today*, October 2011. Available at: http://www.armscontrol.org/act/2011_10/U.S._Chinese_Nuclear_Dialogue.

31 Nuclear Posture Review Report, 2010, http://www.defense.gov/npr/docs/2010%20nuclear%20posture%20review%20report.pdf.

32 Michael Chase has argued that these debates resulted in a reaffirmation that 'peace and development remained the main theme of the times', although leavened with 'greater concerns about U.S. strategic intentions and a consensus in favor of higher defense spending'. See Chase, 'China's Transition to a More

Credible Nuclear Deterrent', *Asia Policy*, vol. 16, July 2013; David M. Finkelstein, 'China Reconsiders its National Security: "The Great Peace and Development Debate of 1999"', CNA Corporation, December 2000, http://cna.org/sites/default/files/research/D0014464.A1.pdf.

33 Gregory Lewis and Jeffrey Kulacki, 'Understanding the Chinese ASAT Test', Union of Concerned Scientists, http://www.ucsusa.org/nuclear_weapons_and_global_security/international_information/us_china_relations/understanding-chinas-asat.html.

34 Annual Report to Congress: Military Power of the People's Republic of China 2006, http://www.defense.gov/pubs/pdfs/China%20Report%202006.pdf.

35 The translated title of the article was 'PRC Expert Warns PRC May Renounce "No-First-Use" of Nuclear Weapons in War Time', with the actual title being 'PRC Expert: China's Policy on Nuclear Weapons Remains Unchanged'. Chu did admit that he could not anticipate every circumstance, but the overall tone of the article was unequivocal, stating that 'there isn't the slightest indication that China's government will let go of this promise', quoting Chu saying he had 'not heard any leader on any occasion state China will change or let go of this position. Never.' Available at http://boxun.com/news/gb/china/2005/07/200507181307.shtml.

36 'The Diversified Employment of China's Armed Forces', Xinhua, 16 April 2013, http://news.xinhuanet.com/english/china/2013-04/16/c_132312681.htm.

37 Speech by Qi Jianguo, 'New Trends in Asia-Pacific Security', 2 June 2013, Singapore, at IISS Shangri-La Dialogue, http://www.iiss.org/en/events/shangri%20la%20dialogue/archive/shangri-la-dialogue-2013-c890/fourth-plenary-session-of17/qa-57d8.

38 For an explication of Chinese nuclear strategy, see Sun Xiangli, 'Analysis of China's Nuclear Strategy', *China Security*, Autumn 2005, pp. 23–27, https://web.archive.org/web/20081120194327/http://www.wsichina.org/back1_05.html (English-language version: Sun, '2005 Reports of International Arms Control and Disarmament', China Arms Control And Disarmament Association, World Knowledge Press, Beijing, 2005) and Sun Xiangli, 'Zhongguo Hezhanlüe Xingzhi yu Tedian Fenxi', Zhanlüe Yanjiu, no. 9, 2006, pp. 23–28.

39 'The Diversified Employment of China's Armed Forces'.

40 The initial translation for these operations is 'anti-nuclear deterrence combat'. However, 'counter-nuclear coercion operations' comes closer to the intended meaning. The term is discussed in the 2000 edition of *Science of Campaigns* and the 2004 *Science of Second Artillery Campaigns*.

41 Mark Stokes, 'China's Nuclear Warhead Storage and Handling System', 12 March 2010, http://www.project2049.net/documents/chinas_nuclear_warhead_storage_and_handling_system.pdf.

42 Given China's nuclear policy of no-first-use, and until recently its limited ballistic-missile early-warning capability, Beijing had

assumed it might have to absorb an initial nuclear blow prior to engaging in nuclear counterattack. Nuclear survivability was particularly critical given China's relatively small number of nuclear weapons and the development by potential adversaries of modern, precision munitions. In recent years, advanced construction design has allowed militaries to go deeper underground to complicate adversarial targeting. For a description of China's network of underground sites for the Second Artillery, see *Annual Report to Congress: Military and Security Developments Involving the People's Republic of China 2011*, p. 36, http://www.defense.gov/pubs/pdfs/2011_cmpr_final.pdf.

43 James Acton, 'The Dragon Dance: U.S.-China Security Cooperation', Carnegie, 29 November 2012, http://carnegieendowment.org/globalten/?fa=50148. See also Lora Saalman, 'China and the U.S. Nuclear Posture Review', The Carnegie Papers (Beijing: Carnegie-Tsinghua Center for Global Policy, 2011), p. 9, http://carnegieendowment.org/files/china_posture_review.pdf.

44 As a part of the discussion surrounding the 2013 White Paper, Yao Yunzhu, director of China's Academy of Military Science, specifically noted: 'The United States is developing a series of conventional strategic strike capabilities. Once deployed, they could have the capability to strike China's nuclear arsenal and make China's NFU policy redundant.' See Yao Yunzhu, 'China Will Not Change Its Nuclear Policy', China US Focus, 22 April 2013, http://www.chinausfocus.com/peace-security/china-will-not-change-its-no-first-use-policy/.

CHAPTER TWO

Nuclear-weapons design and testing

China's current nuclear forces consist of thermonuclear warheads with large yields. This includes multi-megaton yield thermonuclear warheads developed for the DF-3, -4 and -5 ballistic missiles, and at least one several hundred kilotonne (kt) yield warhead developed in the 1990s for China's current generation of solid-fuelled ballistic missiles. These warheads probably make relatively inefficient use of plutonium in the primary to reduce the amount of explosives in, and therefore mass of, the warhead. Chinese designers worked hard to miniaturise the country's warheads, yet China's most modern warhead is unlikely to be small enough for more than one to be placed on China's current generation of solid-fueled ballistic missiles.

Since its first nuclear explosion in 1964, China has developed only a small number of warhead designs. Although there is some question about this number, China tested a 15kt device in 1966; a 3-megatonne (mt) device in the early 1970s for the DF-3 and possibly DF-4 missiles; a 4–5mt nuclear device in the 1970s and 1980s for the DF-5 missile; and a several hundred-kilotonne warhead in the 1990s for China's solid-fuelled missiles, including the DF-21 and DF-31. China also developed an enhanced radiation warhead (ERW) during the early 1980s, but does not appear to have deployed it.

These warheads are based on a relatively small number of nuclear tests. China conducted 45 nuclear tests, most of which were carried out during the period before China's reform under Deng Xiaoping. China stopped nuclear-explosive testing after signing the Comprehensive Nuclear-Test-Ban Treaty (CTBT) in 1996. China probably conducts subcritical tests and other stockpile stewardship measures to ensure the viability of its nuclear-weapons designs. It is unclear whether China periodically remanufactures its warheads, as Russia does, although the Chinese warhead-handling system would seem to imply that China periodically replaces its stockpile.[1] Chinese leaders always emphasised the importance of thermonuclear weapons and ballistic missiles. Among the early documents related to the Chinese nuclear-weapons programme, guidance issued by the Central Committee in 1958 committed China to developing ballistic missiles and high-yield thermonuclear warheads. Unlike other nuclear powers, China conducted very few tests to develop deliverable fission devices, moving quickly instead to develop thermonuclear weapons.

China's emphasis on the development of a small number of large-yield thermonuclear weapons reflects the strategic rationale outlined by the head of China's nuclear-weapons programme, Nie Rongzhen, in 1961. Rather than seeking the development of many fission devices that could be used to practical effect on a battlefield, Nie emphasised the need for a strategic retaliatory capability that would establish China's position in the world and serve as China's scientific and technological base.

Another theme emerges: the attention paid to politics by Chinese weaponeers. The most curious case is China's costly development of an ERW in the 1980s only to shelve it as Beijing had previously done with the aircraft-delivered fission device tested in 1965. The initiation of a programme to develop a neutron bomb starting in the late 1970s and the return to warhead modernisation in the mid-1980s suggest the importance of politics in securing resources for China's strategic programmes.

The story of China's nuclear-weapons programme is one of slow progress in search of missile-deliverable high-yield weapons. According to official Chinese accounts, China's first generation of deliverable nuclear weapons was developed from the early 1970s to the mid-1980s. This would suggest a later time frame than US estimates, which were largely based on correlating missile deployments with tests. There is a strong circumstantial case that China did not produce a satisfactory warhead for either the DF-4 or DF-5 ICBM until the late 1980s, or even the early 1990s.[2] Moreover, the limited information would suggest that China was extremely conservative in its design choices. China shifted to plutonium as the primary fissile material in its nuclear weapons after the late 1960s and appeared to use more plutonium per warhead than other advanced nuclear powers.

Increased use of plutonium is one way to reduce the amount of high explosive in, and so reduce the mass of, nuclear weapons. Chinese primaries probably use on average more plutonium than the approximately 4 kilogrammes (kg) per warhead found in US nuclear weapons. One finding suggests that the primary might contain as much as 7kg, although with a significant level of uncertainty.[3] This has important implications for our assessment of China's nuclear-weapons potential. If China produced less than two tonnes of plutonium, but uses an average of 6kg in each warhead, then its total stockpile could not exceed about 300 warheads.[4] The possibility that China is, for now, plutonium-constrained is significant, if not widely appreciated.

China's nuclear-testing history

Existing histories have largely emphasised the process leading to China's first fission and thermonuclear devices.[5] John Lewis and Xue Litai's *China Builds the Bomb* is excellent and remains definitive despite the flood of Chinese material that has become available since its publication. The period following China's development of a workable staged thermonuclear device is, however, less well understood.

A lack of direct statements regarding the purpose of individual tests makes it difficult to determine their purpose. Chinese accounts emphasise successful events that represent the culmination of research. Histories omit failures unless in the service of some larger narrative culminating in success.

That said, Chinese documentary sources, particularly biographies of individual scientists, provide a surprising amount of detail about the general direction of the development of the nuclear-weapons programmes. Although these accounts are less detailed about China's final series of tests during the 1990s, they chart the development of the programme through the development of an ERW in the 1980s.

These accounts can be compared with declassified US assessments of China's nuclear-weapons testing, particularly from the period 1964–72 and again from 1992–96. Moreover, declassified estimates can be better understood using open-source technical information relating to radiochemical and seismic analysis.

Finally, a surprising amount of information about US assessment of China's nuclear-weapons programmes is available in press accounts relating to allegations of Chinese espionage. For example, several sources describe a Chinese scientist stating during a talk at Los Alamos that China was developing aspherical primaries for thermonuclear weapons – a classified design concept in the US.[6]

During the 1990s, the US believed it had a general sense of the direction of Chinese testing, but was not able to confidently assign a primary purpose to individual tests. Instead it attempted to infer purpose from overall trends in China's nuclear-testing programme.

This chapter undertakes a similar exercise, using Chinese historical sources, declassified intelligence assessments and open-source seismic and radiochemistry data. Uncertainties still remain, specifically about whether China's final series of tests included efforts to incorporate insensitive high explosives (IHE) into China's stockpile and when China completed development of the warhead for the DF-5 ICBM.

China's early nuclear-weapons designs

The most important point in China's nuclear-weapons development is the 1961 decision to continue the nuclear-weapons programme in the face of continuing economic turmoil and the suspension of Soviet assistance. The Soviet Union had agreed to supply China with significant design information, including a prototype nuclear weapon. Once Chinese leaders realised that this assistance would not be forthcoming, an argument ensued about whether to continue the programme. Nie won this argument and consolidated resources behind a reconfigured nuclear-weapons programme.

This decision resulted in the surprising move to pursue a first nuclear explosion using highly enriched uranium (HEU) in an implosion configuration. China's leaders made a commitment to pursue the production of HEU in order to meet the initial goal of conducting a test by the end of 1964 because the gaseous diffusion plant at Lanzhou was much nearer to completion than the plutonium production reactor and reprocessing line at Jiuquan.

China's weaponeers, however, sought multi-megaton thermonuclear weapons, which use a fission device as a primary (staged thermonuclear weapons comprise a primary and secondary stage). As a result, they selected the more technically complex implosion method, rather than a gun-type design, since an implosion device would be necessary to serve as a primary in a thermonuclear warhead for China's future ballistic-missile force.

The Chinese decision to pursue uranium implosion resulted in considerable confusion within the US intelligence community, which detected preparations for a nuclear explosion in the Gobi Desert near Lop Nor, but not for the production of fissile material. There was a widespread expectation that China would pursue the plutonium route using a yet-to-be identified reactor. Meanwhile, analysts had incorrectly assessed the gaseous diffusion plant at Lanzhou as being too small to produce HEU and not yet operational. The apparent incongruity of preparations for a nuclear explosion with no ready source fissile material confused the US intelligence community to the end. An August 1964 memo made note of the apparent paradox, then, in a footnote, deferred the question to a Special National Intelligence Assessment scheduled for November.[7] By then China had conducted its first nuclear explosion using HEU.

China's first nuclear device – code-named 596 after the date of the June 1959 letter suspending Soviet assistance to China's nuclear industry – was too heavy to serve as an operational weapon. Images from the October 1964 test show it being rolled to the test tower. Thereafter, China moved quickly to test a smaller device that could be delivered by an aircraft (CHIC-2), completing the test in May 1965.[8] China had developed plans for such a weapon during the early 1960s. In this period, however, China's aircraft industry had suffered with other conventional-force modernisation programmes as Nie Ronghzen succeeded in consolidating China's limited resources behind the development of ballistic missiles and thermonuclear weapons. Immediately after the successful test in May 1965, the Special Committee abandoned trial production of the aircraft-delivered warhead, shifting to the development of thermonuclear weapons.[9] The second Chinese nuclear explosion might have been the final Chinese test of a weaponised version of the uranium implosion device, but doubts soon arose over the question of whether China's nuclear-warhead design was rugged enough to survive the extremes of temperature, shock and vibration associated with a journey aboard a ballistic missile.

By some accounts the fourth nuclear-weapons test was to be China's first underground test, undertaken to validate the design of the missile-delivered device and to confirm principles related to underground testing, with a view to moving all future tests underground. However, China's weaponeers had concerns about the reliability of China's first missile-delivered warhead. Their US counterparts, too, had debated whether or not it would be necessary to launch a live nuclear weapon on a ballistic missile to be confident that the warhead could survive the journey.[10] China's nuclear weaponeers initially believed that 'cold' tests using warhead mockups would suffice, but they eventually pressed for testing a missile with a live warhead.[11] Thus China's fourth test was an unusual above-ground test of a nuclear warhead launched by a ballistic missile. The decision appears to have been driven by both technical factors – concern that ground tests could not accurately simulate the conditions during flight – and political factors. Some recent Chinese accounts suggest that China wished to convince the Johnson administration that Beijing possessed an operational nuclear capability.[12] China's political leaders were reluctant to authorise the test of a nuclear weapon on a ballistic missile. Zhou Enlai sent the weaponeers back to review plans in December 1965. Nie persuaded Zhou in March 1966 to authorise the 'two in one' test.[13] The preparations for the test were unusually involved. China conducted a number of DF-2 tests with dummy warheads and outfitted the warhead with a self-destruct mechanism. China launched the DF-2A on 27 October at 9am. The missile flew for nine minutes and 14 seconds over 1,000km before exploding with a force of 12kt over the Lop Nor test site (CHIC-4). The Khan network would later provide this design to Libya, having first obtained it from China in the early 1980s.[14] China's first underground test would not occur until September 1969 with CHIC-11. (See Box: China's Drive toward underground nuclear testing.)

China develops thermonuclear weapons

With the successful demonstration of a missile-carried nuclear warhead in 1966, China turned back toward the development of a thermonuclear weapon. (In modern staged thermonuclear weapons, a fission device serves as a primary, with the radiation from the nuclear explosion compressing a secondary of thermonuclear fuel.) Although it was the fifth country to conduct a nuclear explosion – following in order the US, the Soviet Union, the UK and France – China was the fourth to test a thermonuclear device, beating France by a little more than a year. The timing may be of little technical significance, but the evident pride of Chinese weaponeers is telling.

The third Chinese nuclear-weapons test used thermonuclear material, but it was not a staged thermonuclear device in which radiation from a fission device implodes a secondary. Debris from CHIC-3 suggests the design was a 'layer cake', called a 'Sloika' in Russian or 'Alarm Clock' in the US.[15]

Chinese scientists did not discover the principle of radiation implosion – the core secret behind the Teller–Ulam design for staged thermonuclear weapons – until late 1965.[22] The fifth

China's Drive toward underground nuclear testing

Testing nuclear weapons underground – either in tunnels dug horizontally into a mountainside or a shaft dug vertically into the ground – offers a number of advantages. A successful underground test will trap the debris underground, reducing the environmental consequences of a nuclear explosion and denying foreign states the ability to analyse fallout. Perhaps most important, underground nuclear tests can result in better data collection, allowing a state to learn more from each test.

China sought to move its testing underground relatively early in its nuclear programme. By some accounts, China intended its fourth nuclear test to be underground before other objectives, including demonstration of a missile-delivered fission device and a breakthrough in thermonuclear-weapon design, took priority.[16] China conducted its first underground nuclear explosion in a tunnel on 22 September 1969 (CHIC-9). Although Chinese sources describe the test as successful, China did not conduct additional tests underground until October 1975 (CHIC-17) and October 1976 (CHIC-20). Some sources suggest that China struggled with instrumentation, conducting tests at reduced yields and the relatively high water table at Lop Nor.

As a result, most of China's nuclear-weapons tests before 1980 were dropped from aircraft to reduce the fallout and resulting political consequences of atmospheric testing. China retrofitted an H-6 bomber in 1963 and an H-5 bomber in 1967, and modified several Q-5 fighter aircraft in 1970 to serve as test assets.[17] Chinese leaders also considered these test assets as available for use in operational missions, in the event of an emergency.[18] Conducting atmospheric tests using aircraft creates other challenges, including the risk of aircraft crashes and accidents. In 1979, for example, a parachute failed in an air-dropped nuclear test.[19] The device landed eight kilometres from the test site, breaking apart on impact. The dispersal of material, as well as the fact that some components sank into the terrain with the force of impact, complicated clean-up efforts[20] China moved testing underground after 1980, announcing in 1984 that it would no longer conduct atmospheric tests.

The major challenge for underground testing is conducting scaled-yield explosive tests – tests where the yield of the device is scaled down from the full yield of the weapon to be deployed. The US and Soviet Union, for example, agreed to a Threshold Test Ban Treaty (TBBT) that prohibited nuclear-weapons tests at yields above 150kt. By some estimates, both parties could confidently develop weapons with yields of up to 500kt, under the 150kt test threshold.[21] China's final series of tests for the DF-31 warhead in the 1990s had an average yield of about 100kt, suggesting the yield of the deployed device may be in the 500kt range.

Chinese test, on 28 December 1966 (CHIC-5), was a test of the radiation implosion principle, followed by a staged-thermonuclear weapon test in June 1967 (CHIC-6).

These devices used HEU in their primaries, rendering them too large for delivery by a ballistic missile and so ill-suited for miniaturisation.

China's seventh test (CHIC-7) was probably a failure. The device had a relatively small yield – approximately 20kt – but the debris contained some thermonuclear materials suggesting an issue with the primary. Failures of early thermonuclear weapons are not unusual; the first US thermonuclear tests of a design by what would become the Lawrence Livermore National Laboratory was a failure.[23] It is generally accepted that testing is essential to develop deliverable thermonuclear weapons.

China tries to miniaturise

Following the seventh nuclear test, China's nuclear-weapons programme entered a period of transition. Plutonium was now available, initially in modest amounts, helping Chinese weaponeers to reduce the size of the primary, replacing HEU with plutonium and mastering the use of deuterium-tritium gas to boost nuclear explosions. The eighth test on 27 December 1968 (CHIC-8) involved the first use of plutonium. It exploded with a force of 3mt. This test was followed by two more of a similar design (CHIC-10 and -11).

The twelfth test, on November 18, 1971 (CHIC-12), was a boosted plutonium primary, using only a small amount of HEU. It represents the transition to efforts to develop the basic thermonuclear-weapons design for deployment on the DF-3, which was one of China's first generation of ballistic missiles.

China appears to have developed a 3mt warhead for the DF-3 with a series of tests through 1974 (CHIC-12, -13, -14, -15 and -16).

China completed development of its warheads much later than assumed. It is possible that Chinese designers did not produce a satisfactory nuclear warhead for the country's ballistic-missile force until the mid-1980s, and according to Chinese sources, the deployment of the first generation of nuclear-armed ballistic missiles was not complete until May 1995.[24] By the mid-1970s, China's weaponeers were attempting to miniaturise China's warheads, most likely for the DF-4 and DF-5. Yu Min, the scientist who led this effort, recalls difficulties in miniaturising primaries, noting that the first smaller primaries had 'serious deficiencies' that made them 'unsuitable' for weaponisation.[25] Tests during this period in the mid-1970s (CHIC-17, -18, -19 and -20) may represent unsatisfactory efforts to further miniaturise China's nuclear warheads.

It appears that China struggled with boosting – the use of deuterium and tritium to make more efficient use of fissile material.[26] Modelling the effects of boosting remains, to this day, one of the last thermonuclear reactions that is difficult to accomplish from first principles. The US has benchmark data from more than 1,000 nuclear tests to approximate the behaviour of boost gases, something that would have been much harder for China with a relatively small number of nuclear tests.

According to Lewis and Xue, China struggled during this period to replace its first generation of neutron initiators, which were made of polonium and beryillum and placed in the centre of the pit.[27] As part of the transition to boosted weapons, the US developed external neutron generators using pulse-neutron tubes. China did not develop a pulse-neutron tube until the mid- to late 1970s, a sign of its relatively slow progress toward modern thermonuclear weapons.[28] Some sources describe CHIC-21 as a new Chinese nuclear-weapons design. The test received unusual attention from the Xinhua News Agency and probably represented the transition to a miniaturised DF-5 warhead. This device showed boosting and an external neutron generator in a reasonably modern fashion.

The fallout data from this test are interesting. Robert Liefer and Lawrence Toonkel estimate that CHIC-21 injected 260 kilocuries of Sr-90 into the atmosphere.[29] According to analysis by Lars-Erik De Geer, this would imply China had used more than 7kg of plutonium in the primary.[30] This is a very large amount. The first US nuclear weapon to use plutonium, Fat Man, contained 6.2kg of plutonium in its primary. Modern US thermonuclear weapons use an average of 4kg, suggesting that many nuclear-weapons designs use less.[31] The total amount may not be 7kg – the uncertainty from such a calculation is about 2kg – but it seems clear that the Chinese in 1976 were using far more plutonium per primary than the US. One possibility is that China used relatively large amounts of plutonium as a method to reduce the overall size of the weapon. The fission primary of a thermonuclear weapon is largely conventional explosion by mass, meaning that efforts to reduce the size and weight of the device usually focus on developing more efficient techniques for imploding the sphere of plutonium. If efforts to reduce the amount of high explosives come at the expense of an efficient compression of plutonium, one solution is to add more plutonium.[32] Following a series of relatively small tests of 20kt or less that may have been part of the development of the primary (CHIC-22 to -25), and a failed test in September 1979 (CHIC-26), China tested a 1mt device in the atmosphere on 16 October 1980 (CHIC-27). This is believed to be an atmospheric proof test of the 5mt warhead for the DF-5 and turned out to be China's final nuclear explosion in the atmosphere.

Two poems: China develops a neutron bomb (1977–1988)

As China's nuclear weaponeers struggled to reduce the size of China's thermonuclear weapons, they faced a new challenge – a directive from the top leadership that China should develop an ERW, better known as a neutron bomb.[33] On 6 June 1977, Walter Pincus published a story in the *Washington Post* detailing the Carter administration's plan to seek funding for a 'killer neutron warhead', the W-70 Mod 3, in the 1978 Energy Research and Development Administration budget.[34] An ERW is simply a thermonuclear weapon with a very small primary (in terms of explosive yield) and a secondary optimised to produce prompt radiation.

Although such a design was not new, the press reports prompted popular opposition. In particular, the Soviet Union launched a vigorous propaganda campaign, referring to the ERW as the 'perfect capitalist bomb' because it would kill people while leaving property intact.

Chinese leaders would have been aware of these stories. The Xinhua News Agency prepared for them summaries of Western press stories, documents known as 'internal reference materials'. The Chinese press carried factual accounts of Pincus's articles and the neutron bomb, but without condemning the weapon as the Soviets had done.[35] Instead of condemnation, biographical accounts of China's most important scientists seem to confirm that China began its own ERW program sometime in 1977, most likely in response to Western press reports about the weapon.[36] On 21 September 1977, Zhang Aiping published a poem in the *Renmin Ribao* (*People's Daily*) that seemed to indicate China's interest in ERWs:

> Steel alloys are not strong, and
> Neutron bombs are not difficult.
> When heroes study the sciences intensely,
> They can storm all earth's strategic passes.[37]

The next day the *People's Daily* carried another short, factual article describing the ERW's features.[38]

The decision to build an ERW seems to have come from the leadership, which now included Deng Xiaoping. In the summer of 1977, Deng was consolidating power.[39] When describing why China sought to develop an ERW one scientist referenced Deng, recalling an earlier remark dating to 1966: 'What others have already done, we also must do; what others have not yet done, we certainly must also do.'[40] There is evidence that some of China's weaponeers were not eager to embrace the neutron bomb. Their reluctance is understandable; China was struggling to miniaturise its nuclear weapons. Developing an ERW would be a technically challenging distraction.

By 1978, however, the National Defense Science and Technology Commission had instructed China's weaponeers to conduct initial research on a 'second generation' of nuclear weapons, including miniaturised weapons and the neutron bomb. The Chinese scientist placed in charge of the ERW programme, Yu Min, felt significant pressure.[41] A biographical account describes a conversation between Yu and a colleague at the China Academy of Sciences (CAS), who expressed concern about Yu's health and suggested he change jobs.

There is other evidence that China was reluctant to develop a neutron bomb. Liu Huaqiu, at the time a senior specialist at the Commission of Science, Technology and Industry for National Defense (COSTIND), wrote a report in 1979 called 'A Review of the Neutron Bomb'.[42] Liu would later author a 1988 monograph as a visiting scholar at Stanford that made a number of arguments about why China did not find an ERW useful.[43] Ultimately, nuclear-weapons scientists acquiesced to political realities. Deng was moving to reduce defence spending, consolidating what little money remained in modernising conventional forces. If China's weaponeers wanted to ensure funding for a second generation of nuclear weapons, they could not afford to ignore the preferences of the top leadership. Xue Bencheng noted the necessity of 'stressing politics' for nuclear-weapons programmes and testing.[44] 'For conducting China's nuclear tests', Xue explained, 'funding was not easy to come by. Use of funds required political foresight, and bearing responsibility to the party and people.'[45]

China's weaponeers may have concluded that an ERW could be developed as part of a broader process of reducing the size of the primaries for China's nuclear weapons.[46] During this period, China sought to improve miniaturisation, mobility, penetrability, safety and reliability.[47] China attempted to use single tests to achieve several of these objectives.[48] For example, after the 4 May 1983 nuclear test, technicians for the first time drilled rapidly into the testing area to obtain radioactive samples for analysis.[49] China appears to have carried out six tests between 1982 to 1988 related to the development of an ERW (CHIC-28–32, and CHIC-34; CHIC-33 is probably related to a different series).[50] According to one scientist, China took a phased approach of testing principles and components before assembling a complete device.[51] Both Yu Min and Deng Jiaxian, who is generally described as the 'father' of China's nuclear weapons designs, emphasised the importance of the 1984 principles test (CHIC-32) as a 'breakthrough' in ERW development. Deng, like Zhang Aiping, wrote a poem to commemorate this test, which was the last he participated in:

> The red cloud attacks the highest heavens,
> and a thousand nuclear forces rock the earth.
> After twenty years of hard climbing,
> the second generation of light boats has passed the bridge.[52]

Following a pause in testing that would last until 1987, China tested an ERW in 1988 (CHIC-34).[53]

China's modern warheads

By the mid-1980s, China's weaponeers were facing a number of bureaucratic challenges. As China underwent a period of reform, funds for defence were increasingly less available and directed mainly to conventional modernisation. China's weaponeers had preserved access by pursuing an ERW in the late 1970s, but with the successful principles test this programme was coming to an end.

Life, too, was beginning to intervene. China's first generation of cadres was growing old. Nie Rongzhen retired, followed by his protégé Zhang Aiping. The new generation of leadership lacked the influence of these men.

In 1984, Deng Jiaxian was diagnosed with cancer. At this point, China's testing programme entered a period of prolonged inactivity. Deng composed a report with Yu Min which argued for a new round of nuclear development.[54] The core of the Deng–Yu letter was that China must resume its efforts to miniaturise warheads before the imposition of a ban on testing. The report represents a transition in the bureaucratic rationale for China's nuclear-weapons programme, closing the door on the ERW programme in favour of completing China's process of warhead miniaturisation.

During this period, veterans of China's strategic industries were moving to ensure funding, despite a growing sense that the model pursued by Nie had produced few benefits. A quartet of leaders sought to ensure funding for the strategic community, and succeeded in getting a letter into Deng Xiaoping's hands advocating the goals of the programme.[55] China created the '863' programme, so called because it was established in March 1986 (86/3 in Chinese formatting), to stimulate the development of advanced technologies in a range of fields.

During the last half of the 1980s and into the early 1990s, China conducted several relatively large tests (CHIC-33, -36 and -37) that may have been final tests for the DF-5 and other ICBMs. Although the general assessment is that China deployed the DF-5 with a warhead atmospherically tested in 1980, the very high yield of the May 1992 test suggests China continued to develop the warhead for the DF-5 through the early 1990s.[56] This device might have made more efficient use of China's stockpile of plutonium, integrating the advances pioneered during the development of the ERW in the early 1980s.

China also began development of the warhead for the DF-21 and DF-31 during the late 1980s and early 1990s. Original plans called for a common warhead across China's solid-fuelled missiles, reported as either a 500kg device with a 200–300kt yield or a 600kg warhead with a 400kt yield.[57] China tested the primary for this device in September 1992 (CHIC-38). Chinese designers had indicated in public that they were developing 'aspherical' primaries – oblate-shaped primaries that allowed designers to reduce the width of the warhead, while making other efforts to reduce the overall weight.

The test series from 1992 to 1996 (CHIC-39 to CHIC-44) validated this warhead. The yield, based on seismic data, clusters around a body-wave magnitude (Mb) of 5.9, corresponding to a yield of about 100kt.[58] (Body-wave magnitudes are also used to measure earthquakes at long distances.) Explosive tests in this range can allow for the development of much larger warheads, perhaps up to 500kt in yield. Nuclear-weapons designers can scale the size of the nuclear tests by substituting secondaries that result in smaller explosions while still validating the weapons design. For example, after the US and the Soviet Union brought into force the TTBT banning explosive

Multiple warheads

The issue of whether China will deploy multiple warheads on its ballistic missiles is complicated by the fact that placing multiple warheads on a missile may require either a larger missile, smaller warheads, or both. At the moment, only China's liquid-fuelled DF-5 ICBM is believed to be large enough to carry more than one of China's smallest warheads, the 470kg reentry vehicle (RV) made for the DF-31 missile.

The US intelligence community believes China may be developing a new road-mobile ICBM that can carry multiple warheads.[59] It's unclear whether this estimate presumes China will also develop a smaller warhead than the DF-31-type RV. About half the throw-weight of an ICBM is lost to the 'post-boost vehicle' that is necessary to carry several warheads. Even Russia's most modern solid-fuelled missiles (such as the SS-27, with a throw-weight of 1,200kg) would have trouble accommodating multiple DF-31-type RVs.[60] It is difficult to credit press reports that say China's next ICBM will carry as many as ten RVs (the massive US *Peacekeeper*, at 3,950kg, could not carry ten Chinese RVs).

China could design smaller warheads, although these would not have the benefit of explosive testing, which China stopped in 1996 after signing the CTBT. Given the limited number of designs in China's arsenal and the small number of tests to provide benchmark data, China would probably struggle to develop warheads in the challenging design space of a few hundred kilotonnes of yield with a few hundred kilogrammes of RV mass, as the US has done with the thermonuclear W76 warhead. China would sacrifice significant yield, reliability or both.

On the other hand, the DF-5 ICBM has a significant throw-weight (3,000–3,200kg) that could accommodate a post-boost vehicle and several DF-31-type RVs. China probably remanufactures warheads as a stockpile stewardship measure, but China might choose to retire the older warhead design in favour of an arsenal based solely on the most modern DF-31-type warhead. In that case, the 18 DF-5s would have a significant amount of throw-weight that would be able to carry either penetration aids or additional DF-31-type RVs.

tests with yields in excess of 150kt, outside experts concluded that this would permit the development of new warheads of up to 500kt in yield.[61] Scaling is an important element in moving nuclear-explosive testing underground, given the challenges of containing the largest nuclear explosions.

Leaked US intelligence from the mid-1990s estimates the mass of the DF-31-type RV as 470kg.[62] Yield-to-weight ratios for modern US thermonuclear weapons range from about 0.6 to 1.5kt per kilogramme, with favourable yield-to-weight ratios being easier to achieve at higher yields.[63] A rough estimate for the DF-21 and DF-31 RVs would be a warhead mass of 500kg and a yield of 500kt.

There are unverified reports that the DF-21 or DF-31 may have three 90kt warheads, possibly based on yields of the final test series. This seems unlikely. The US intelligence community assesses that all of China's solid-fuelled missiles carry only a single warhead. China would face many challenges in developing smaller warheads without testing, because it is accepted that the greatest design challenge is to create thermonuclear warheads that weigh less than 200kg while retaining an efficient yield-to-weight ratio (in the 0.5–1.5 range).[64] Not surprisingly, this design space is where current US warheads largely fall.

An open question relates to whether China's most recent design integrates IHE. Declassified US intelligence assessments suggest that China did not stand up a domestic capacity to manufacture IHE until late in the development process for the DF-31-type RV. IHE is less energetic than other explosives used to implode the plutonium pit in a nuclear weapon's primary, resulting in added weight. It is also necessary to validate IHE with explosive tests. Other sources, however, suggest a continuing Chinese interest in integrating IHE into their stockpile.

Following what appears to have been its final test of a DF-31-type RV, China conducted two tests that may have supported further modernisation or stewardship of the stockpile (CHIC-44, CHIC-45). The purpose of these tests, and whether CHIC-44 was two smaller devices detonated at the same time, is unclear.

Stockpile stewardship

China signed the CTBT in 1996. How will China maintain confidence in its stockpile without nuclear testing? The basic view is that China has relatively simple designs that are less likely to suffer unexpected problems. On the other hand, China conducted a small number of nuclear tests and deployed only a few designs. A single serious problem would affect a significant portion of the stockpile. During the 1990s, the US intelligence community believed that China would need to resume testing to validate a replacement design in the event of a serious problem in the stockpile.[65] Given the small number of tests, and their likely purpose, China probably has one modern design developed for the DF-31 and other solid-fuelled missiles tested between 1992 and 1996, as well as one partially tested alternative design concept.

A presentation by a senior Chinese official in 2008 outlined some basic details of China's efforts following the test ban.[66] The approach is largely consistent with US efforts to improve monitoring of existing warheads, make better use of test data and develop new facilities for testing and simulation. China has invested in the same sort of stockpile stewardship facilities as the US, including laser-driven inertial confinement fusion and radiography.

China maintains its nuclear-test site at Lop Nor in a state of apparent readiness. While personnel do not live year round at the site, satellite photographs show that it is kept in good repair.[67] China also appears to conduct subcritical tests at the Lop Nor site.[68]

China stopped nuclear-explosive testing after signing the CTBT in 1996. The Comprehensive Nuclear-Test-Ban Treaty Organization's (CTBTO's) International Monitoring System (IMS) is capable of detecting explosions at yields below those necessary to develop new warhead designs at Lop Nor. The current IMS can with a high degree of confidence detect yields as low as 3.4 Mb, which roughly correspond to 90 tonnes.[69] The US has its own classified monitoring system, the Atomic Energy Detection System (AEDS).[70] Declassified estimates in the mid-1990s suggested the AEDS could monitor explosions that corresponded to a few hundred tonnes.[71] US capabilities have likely improved since then.[72]

A major development in recent years is the dramatic improvement in supercomputing in China. Nuclear-weapons programmes make extensive use of supercomputers because the codes for modelling thermonuclear explosions are extraordinarily complicated. Over the past two decades, the fastest supercomputer in the world has usually been located at one of the US nuclear-weapons laboratories such as Los Alamos, Lawrence Livermore or Oak Ridge. During the US debate over ratification of the CTBT, a significant question was whether supercomputing targets were realistic.

China's supercomputers during this period were improving, albeit far behind the US and well below the goals that US national laboratories set for maintaining confidence under a test ban. During the 1990s, US intelligence closely watched China's development of supercomputers, which remained several generations behind their American counterparts.[73] Today, the Tianhe-2 developed by China's National University of Defense Technology has surpassed Titan at Oak Ridge National Laboratory as the fastest supercomputer in the world.[74] China is now at computing parity with the US, with capabilities in excess of the requirements outlined by US national laboratories in the late 1990s to maintain the stockpile under the test ban.

Fast supercomputers do not substitute for data from testing and qualified personnel. Still, much-improved supercomputers combined with a programme of subcritical testing most likely increase China's options to deal with ageing or other problems that may arise in its nuclear stockpile. These tools might also permit Chinese designers more freedom to develop new warheads.

Historically, US nuclear-weapons designers have been reluctant to rely on designs that were not tested. Chinese designers appear to have been even more conservative than their US counterparts. Ultimately, however, the issue is one of preference and generational change. Younger scientists and engineers are simply more comfortable with computer simulations. The degree to which Chinese weaponeers feel free to deviate from simple designs developed before 1996 is ultimately a question of organisational culture and confidence.

Allegations of espionage

A major question about the development of China's nuclear-weapons programme has been the role of espionage and foreign assistance. The history of nuclear weapons is intertwined with a history of espionage, starting with Klaus Fuchs, the Rosenbergs and other Soviet spies who compromised the Manhattan Project. Assessing the impact of atomic espionage is challenging because spies steal ideas. For example, a major question concerns how the Soviets discovered the concept of radiation implosions. Did they learn about it from a spy such as Fuchs, discover it through analysis of debris from US tests in the Pacific or simply reach the same conclusion as US designers?[75] Some accounts indicate that China 'stole' or otherwise acquired US nuclear-weapons designs. There is no evidence to support this characterisation. Careful sources refer instead to 'design information' – a general term that references concepts relating to the design of a nuclear weapon. While there are plausible reasons to protect nuclear-weapons design information from public disclosure, the compromise of such information would not substitute for a country's indigenous design capabilities or the data gathered from nuclear-weapons testing and simulations.

The major issue relates to a document provided by a walk-in to the American Institute in Taiwan (AIT) in 1995 that contained a number of details about nuclear weapons in the US stockpiles. The walk-in document appears to have been a product of China's missile industry, not its nuclear-weapons design academy, using US nuclear weapons as rough technological benchmarks for the design of RVs.[76] This is the sort of information that was later compromised in 2006, when the Air Force inadvertently shipped *Minuteman* III nose cones to Taiwan.

'Design information' in, for example, the case of the US W88 warhead, refers to a 'crude sketch' that contained the following classified concepts: that the W88 has an aspherical primary; that the primary is placed forward rather than aft in the warhead; and the diameter of the primary and secondary.[77] Some of the design information in the 'walk-in' document was correct, but other details were wrong and reportedly based on open sources.[78] To complicate the matter further, the US later determined that the walk-in had been under the control of Chinese intelligence services. Despite concerns about accuracy and provenance, the details contained in the document led to the espionage allegations that dominated the debate about China's nuclear modernisation during the 1990s.

A close look at the major cases relating to Chinese nuclear espionage illustrates how little evidence links allegations of espionage to specific developments in China's nuclear-weapons programme. The earliest case dates to 1981. The Cox Committee and other official publications have asserted that China acquired design information relating to the ERW.[79] The design information in question is an answer to what has been described as 'a general physics question', as well as another question relating to the concept of two-point implosion.[80] The questions were reportedly found on an index card that Gwo-Bao Min, an aeronautical engineer employed by Livermore's then D-Division, used to prepare a lecture he delivered in China in 1981. Years later, some US analysts surmised that the answer to the question could have been of use in developing ERWs. Min resigned from Livermore, but was not charged with criminal wrongdoing. He continued to travel to China.[81] In a later case, Peter Lee, an employee of Los Alamos National Laboratory and the US corporation TRW, gave technical lectures in China. Lee discussed his work relating to inertial confinement fusion, including answering a question on deuterium and tritium – gases used to boost nuclear explosions that inertial confinement fusion (ICF) can help model. Lee's work was classified in 1985 when he gave the lecture and then declassified in 1993. Lee pleaded guilty to disclosing information related to his work with lasers in ICF. He was sentenced to a year in a halfway house, community service and a fine.

Finally, there is the well-known case of former Los Alamos employee Wen Ho Lee. In the wake of the 1995 disclosure by the walk-in, Lee fell under suspicion. Investigators claimed they discovered that Lee had downloaded computer codes from a classified system onto an unclassified system, then made copies. Lee also reportedly admitted to not fully disclosing the extent of his contacts with Chinese weaponeers on two visits to China. Still, there was no evidence that Lee passed classified information regarding the W88 or any other warhead to China. Although charged with 59 counts of mishandling classified information relating to his downloading of computer codes, Lee ultimately pleaded guilty to a single felony count of mishandling classified information. He walked out of the courtroom with an apology from the presiding judge.

There is very little evidence that these individuals provided significant assistance to the Chinese nuclear-weapons programme. Only Peter Lee pleaded guilty to compromising information on inertial confinement fusion (ICF), which would be subsequently declassified. Min was never charged and Wen Ho Lee pleaded guilty only to mishandling classified data.

China and the US have certainly spied on one another in an attempt to learn about each other's nuclear programmes. 'From time to time they have been in our kitchen looking for recipes and we have poked around in theirs' is Harold Agnew's colourful characterisation.[82] It is also possible that we do not know the full extent of wrongdoing.

There is also minimal evidence that the compromise of information from the US programme, or from Russian or French programmes for that matter, has altered the general trajectory of China's nuclear-weapons programme. All programmes have benefited from espionage, but it is simply impossible to prove that competent designers in other countries would not have eventually found the correct solution on their own. Design information does not compensate for actual design expertise and nuclear testing to execute conceptual notions, although it may avoid wasteful expenditures on technological dead ends. As Agnew argued: 'Having a computer printout as I remember them would give the general idea, but actually being able to manufacture the total system from a computer code is a different matter.'[83]

Conclusion

China's current stockpile of nuclear weapons probably comprises two thermonuclear-weapon designs tested from the late 1980s through 1996. These designs appear relatively simple and make heavy use of plutonium.

China's most modern warhead, for the DF-31 and other solid-fuelled ballistic missiles, probably weighs about 500kg and may have a yield of about 500kt. This warhead is too large for China to place multiple warheads on its solid-fuelled ballistic missiles, but China might place two or three such warheads on its DF-5 ICBMs.

China would face difficulty in developing a smaller nuclear warhead without testing. Despite having vastly better computers today, China can draw upon data from only 45 nuclear tests, many of which were conducted before the reform and modernisation of China's science and technology base started by Deng Xiaoping. Chinese nuclear-weapons designers appear to have been relatively conservative in their designs.

It is difficult to estimate how much fissile material China uses in each warhead, although a range of 4–6kg may serve as an approximate bound for a nuclear-weapons programme that by ability and preference prefers more conservative designs. By comparison the US averages approximately 4kg of plutonium per warhead. If China uses between 4 and 6kg, its total stockpile of nuclear weapons probably could not exceed several hundred warheads. China almost certainly has enough plutonium to support a modest expansion of its current nuclear arsenal, but a dramatic expansion may well require a new generation of nuclear-weapons designs, a resumption of plutonium production, or both.

Notes

[1] For a primer on China's warhead handling system, see Mark Stokes, 'China's Nuclear Warhead Storage and Handling System', Project 2049 Institute, 12 March 2010, http://www.project2049.net/documents/chinas_nuclear_warhead_storage_and_handling_system.pdf.

[2] The US appears to believe that the DF-3 and DF-4 use the same warhead, while the DF-5 uses a different warhead.

[3] Lars-Erik De Geer, 'The radioactive signature of the hydrogen bomb', Science & Global Security, vol. 2, 1991, pp. 351–63.

[4] The IAEA defines a significant quantity of plutonium as 8kg, which is sufficient for a simple fission device of the sort that a state might manufacture as a first weapon and includes an allowance for the loss of plutonium during processing. 'Fat Man', the device exploded in

Table 1. **China's Nuclear Tests 1964–1996**

CHIC-N	Date	Type	Mb	Yield (kt)	Note
1	16-Oct-64	Atmospheric		22	Simple fission device
2	14-May-65	Atmospheric		40	Aircraft-delivered fission device
3	9-May-66	Atmospheric		300	'Layer cake' thermonuclear device
4	27-Oct-66	Atmospheric		30	Missile-delivered fission device
5	28-Dec-66	Atmospheric		500	Thermonuclear principles test
6	17-Jun-67	Atmospheric		3300	First thermonuclear-weapons test
7	24-Dec-67	Atmospheric		25	Possibly a failure
8	27-Dec-68	Atmospheric		3000	First use of plutonium
9	22-Sep-69	Underground	5.1	7	First underground test
10	29-Sep-69	Atmospheric		3000	
11	14-Oct-70	Atmospheric		3400	
12	18-Nov-71	Atmospheric		20	First use of boosting
13	7-Jan-72	Atmospheric		20	
14	18-Mar-72	Atmospheric		200	Possibly a failure
15	27-Jun-73	Atmospheric		3000	
16	17-Jun-74	Atmospheric		1000	
17	27-Oct-75	Underground	4.8	3	
18	23-Jan-76	Atmospheric		20	
19	26-Sep-76	Atmospheric		200	
20	17-Oct-76	Underground	4.8	3	
21	17-Nov-76	Atmospheric		4000	Possibly a new thermonuclear design
22	17-Sep-77	Atmospheric		20	
23	15-Mar-78	Atmospheric		20	
24	14-Oct-78	Underground	4.5	20	
25	14-Dec-78	Atmospheric		1	
26	13-Sep-79	Failure		0	Parachute did not deploy
27	16-Oct-80	Atmospheric		1000	Final atmospheric test , Possible DF-5 warhead
28	5-Oct-82	Underground		15	Enhanced radiation warhead (ERW)
29	4-May-83	Underground	4	1	ERW
30	6-Oct-83	Underground	5.5	22	ERW
31	3-Oct-84	Underground	5.2	9	ERW
32	19-Dec-84	Underground	4.4	1	ERW principles test
33	5-Jun-87	Underground	6.2	230	Possible scaled DF-5 warhead
34	29-Sep-88	Underground	4.3	1	ERW final test
35	26-May-90	Underground	5.3	12	
36	16-Aug-90	Underground	6.1	170	
37	21-May-92	Underground	6.6	700	
38	25-Sep-92	Underground	4.6	1	Aspherical primary for the DF-31 warhead
39	5-Oct-93	Underground	5.6	70	DF-31 warhead
40	10-Jun-94	Underground	5.7	50	DF-31 warhead
41	7-Oct-94	Underground	5.8	70	DF-31 warhead
42	15-May-95	Underground	6.0	140	DF-31 warhead
43	17-Aug-95	Underground	6.0	100	DF-31 warhead
44	8-Jun-96	Underground	5.7	49	DF-31 warhead
45	29-Jul-96	Underground	4.2	1	Possible primary for a lighter warhead

All yields are approximate. Yields of the atmospheric tests are rounded, from Defense Threat Reduction Agency, Nuclear Explosion Database, available at: http://www.rdss.info/. Mb yields of underground tests, again rounded, are from Aoife O'Mongain, Alan Douglas and John B. Young, 'Body-wave Magnitudes and Locations of Presumed Explosions at the Chinese Test Site, 1967–1996', 22nd Annual DoD/DoE Seismic Research Symposium: Planning for Verification of and Compliance with the Comprehensive Nuclear Test-ban Treaty, New Orleans, LA, 15 September, 2000.

Nagaski in 1945, contained about 6kg of plutonium.

5   *Ibid.*

6   See Ian Hoffman and Dan Stober, *A Convenient Spy: Wen Ho Lee and the Politics of Nuclear Espionage* (New York: Simon & Schuster, 2002), p. 109.

7   CIA, 'The Chances of an Imminent Communist Chinese Nuclear Explosion', Special National Intelligence Estimate, 26 August 1964, approved for release May 2004.

8   For an initial chronology of China's nuclear tests, see Thomas Reed and Danny Stillman, 'The Chinese Nuclear Tests, 1964–1996', *Physics Today*, September 2008.

9   *China Today: Defense Science and Technology,* Volume 1 (Beijing: National Defense Industry Press, 1993) p. 232.

10 Ultimately the US conducted a single test of a W47 nuclear weapon on a *Polaris* missile, fired at reduced range to the Pacific test site in May 1962. The US Navy provides a description of the event, available at http://www.navy.mil/navydata/ cno/n87/usw/issue_24/frigate_ bird2.htm.

11 *China Today: Defense Science and Technology,* pp. 229–30

12 An account in Xinhua in 2009 describes that 'imperialist powers' viewed China's nuclear programme as 'a bullet without a gun' because China did not have a means of delivery at the time of initial nuclear tests. See 'DF-2A Missile Reversed New China's Bullet Without a Gun Situation', Xinhua, 3 April 2009, http:// www.qh.xinhuanet.com/misc/2009- 04/03/content_16147706.htm.

13 *China Today: Defense Science and Technology* , pp. 226-228.

14 One technical feature of the design is the use of a uranium deuteride initiator. Western experts were puzzled by a photograph of Pakistani scientist A.Q. Khan in front of a blackboard with a diagram of a nuclear weapon that included the phrase 'uran- deuteride initiator'. As it turns out, four scientists from the Southwest Institute of Fluid Mechanics in Sichuan published a detailed explanation in a 1989 paper entitled 'Fusion Produced by Implosion of Spherical Explosive'. The paper is included in the proceedings of an American Physical Society meeting published as *Shock Compression of Condensed Matter*, S.C. Schmidt, James N. Johnson, Lee W. Davison (eds), (North-Holland, 1990). See also Jeffrey Lewis, 'Uranium Deuteride Initiators', Arms Control Wonk, 14 December 2009, http://lewis.armscontrolwonk. c o m / a r c h i v e / 2 5 6 7 / uranium-deuteride-initiators.

15 De Geer, 'The radioactive signature of the hydrogen bomb'. A 'layer cake' design is one where fusion occurs from spheres of thermonuclear fuel surrounding the fission core, rather than a 'true' thermonuclear device involving radiation implosion of a physically separate secondary. *Sloika* is usually translated as layer cake.

16 *China Today: Defense Science and Technology*, p. 249.

17 China may have intended to use the bombers for operations in addition to testing: 'In September 1967 the government assigned the task for retrofitting the H-5 into a nuclear

carrier which could be used both for nuclear test and operational missions'; see *China Today: Aviation Industry* (Beijing, China Aviation Industry Press, 1989) pp. 146–47.

18 *China Today: Aviation Industry*, pp. 144, 146 and 155.

19 Deng Jiaxian, *Biographies of the Founders of the Nuclear, Missile, and Satellite Programme* (Beijing: Tsinghua University Press, 2001).

20 For a first-person account of the failed 1979 test by a member of the crew sent to recover the remains of the device, see: http://blog.sina.com. cn/s/blog_71e4f47201018ah4.html.

21 Harold Feiveson, Christopher Paine and Frank von Hippel, 'A Low Threshold Test Ban is Feasible', *Science*, vol. 238, no. 4826, 23 October 1987, p. 458.

22 *China Today: Defense Science and Technology*, pp. 196–97.

23 For a thorough review of early US thermonuclear development and testing, see Chuck Hansen, *Swords of Armageddon: U.S. Nuclear Weapons Development since 1945,* October 1995, Volume III. (1995).

24 Xu J. Niao, *Kan di qiu - zhong guo zhan lue dao dan zhen di gong cheng ji shi* (Beijing: PLA Literature and Art Publishing House, 2006), p. 361.

25 Deng, *Biographies*, pp. 55–63.

26 John Lewis and Xue Litai, *China Builds the Bomb*, (Stanford University Press, 1988) pp. 155–160; and Lewis and Xue, *China's Strategic Seapower: The Politics of Force Modernization in the Nuclear Age* (Stanford University Press, 1996) pp. 177–78.

27 Lewis and Xue, *China's Strategic Seapower*, pp. 177–78.

28 China's first scientific publication on pulse-neutron tubes dates to 1977. See *Huanfa Zhongzi Ce Jing Xiezuo Zu*, 'Huanfa Zhongzi Ce Jing', *Yuanzineng Kexue Jishu*, February 1977.

29 De Geer, 'The radioactive signature of the hydrogen bomb'.

30 Lars-Erik De Geer, 'Chinese Atmospheric Nuclear Explosions from a Swedish Horizon: A Summary of Swedish Observations of Chinese Nuclear Test Explosions in the Atmosphere, 1964–1980', paper prepared for the Scope-Radtest Workshop in Beijing, 19–21 October 1996.

31 The average amount of plutonium in the US stockpile can be obtained by dividing the stockpile of plutonium (46.8 metric tonnes) by the size of the warhead stockpile at the time (approximately 11,100 warheads), giving a result of about 4kg per warhead. See Jeffrey Lewis, 'Grading the NPR on Transparency', Arms Control Wonk, 13 April 2010, http://lewis.armscontrolwonk. c o m / a r c h i v e / 2 6 8 7 / grading-the-npr-transparency.

32 Thomas Cochran and Christopher Paine, 'The Amount of Plutonium and Highly-Enriched Uranium Needed for Pure Fission Nuclear Weapons', Natural Resources Defense Council, 13 April 1995, http://www.nrdc.org/nuclear/ fissionw/fissionweapons.pdf.

33 This section draws heavily on research conducted with Jonathan Ray for his master's thesis. A more complete account can be found in his forthcoming monograph, Jonathan Ray, *Red China's Capitalist Bomb: Inside the PRC's Neutron Bomb Program,* (China Strategic Perspectives, National Defense Univeristy, forthcoming 2014).

[34] Walter Pincus, 'Neutron Killer Warhead Buried in ERDA Budget', *Washington Post*, 6 June 1977 and 'Pentagon Pushes Neutron Shell for Artillery Forces', *Washington Post*, 24 June 1977.

[35] See FBIS, Document ID CHI-77-134, 'Ta Kung Pao Discusses Neutron Bomb Issue', from *Hong Kong Ta Kung Pao*, in Chinese, 9 July 1977, and 'U.S. President Carter Asks Congress to Agree to Neutron Bomb Production', *People's Daily*, 16 July 1977.

[36] Mao Zedong died in September 1976 and the Cultural Revolution ended soon after. Yu Min's recollection is taken from Deng's *Biographies*, pp. 56–63. Yu says the order to develop a 'second generation of nuclear weapons' came in the mid-1970s. He also recalls a conversation with Qian Sanqiang, who had 'come out of retirement', returned to the China Academy of Sciences (CAS) and invited Yu Min to come to CAS. Yu declined the invitation to continue work on the ERW and miniaturisation programmes. Xue Bencheng said in an interview that China began researching ERWs in the 1970s. See FBIS, Document ID CHI-2001-0613, 'PRC Chief Engineer of Neutron Bomb Interviewed on Nuclear Weapons Development', from *Chengdu Sichuan Ribao*, in Chinese, 11 June 2001.

[37] Poem by Zhang Aiping: 'No Limits to What Can Be Climbed – On Reading Marshal Ye's Poem "Storm the Strategic Pass"', *People's Daily*, 21 September 1977. Translation by Jonathan Ray.

[38] 'The Neutron Bomb', *People's Daily*, 22 September 1977.

[39] On 22 July 1977 the Communist Party officially restored Deng to the offices of vice premier of the State Council, vice chairman of the Central Committee, vice chairman of the Military Commission and chief of the General Staff of the PLA.

[40] Chen Junxiang, *China's Unique Path for Developing Nuclear Weapons: The Nuclear, Missile and Satellite Program* (Jiuzhou Press, 2001), p. 157. Chen worked at the Ninth Academy and supported nuclear tests.

[41] Deng, *Biographies*, pp. 56–63.

[42] Liu Huaqing, *A Review of the Neutron Bomb* (China's Defense Science and Technology Information Centre, 1979.) A record of this publication is available at: http://218.249.41.17/was40/detail?record=57961&channelid=10234.

[43] Liu Huaqiu, *China and the Neutron Bomb* (Stanford, CA: Stanford University Press, 1988).

[44] 'Stressing politics' was part of the Communist Party vernacular from 1998 to the early 2000s. Jiang Zemin's 'Three Stress Campaign' emphasised the need for party members to study politics and adapt ideology to changing circumstances.

[45] FBIS, 'PRC Chief Engineer of Neutron Bomb Interviewed on Nuclear Weapons Development'.

[46] Deng, *Biographies*, p. 58.

[47] *China Today; Defense Science and Technology*, p. 223.

[48] Chen, *China's Unique Path for Developing Nuclear Weapons*, pp. 160-161 and FBIS, 'PRC Chief Engineer of Neutron Bomb Interviewed on Nuclear Weapons Development'.

[49] Xie Guang, *Dangdai*, p. 274.

50 *Ibid.*, p. 223.

51 Chen, *China's Unique Path for Developing Nuclear Weapons*, pp. 160–61.

52 Translation by Jonathan Ray. Poem appears in Yu Min, *Biographies of the Founders of the Nuclear, Missile, and Satellite Program* (Beijing: Tsinghua University Press, 2001), as well as in numerous news articles and biographies on Deng Jiaxian.

53 'Facts Speak Louder Than Words and Lies Will Collapse by Themselves – Further Refutation of the Cox Report', People's Republic of China, Information Office of the State Council, 15 July 1999.

54 Min, *Biographies*, pp. 56–63.

55 For a history of the 863 programme, see Evan A. Feigenbaum, *China's Techno-Warriors: National Security and Strategic Competition from the Nuclear to the Information Age* (Stanford, CA: Stanford University Press, 2003), pp. 141–88.

56 An alternate possibility is that the yields lie at the low end of the range of uncertainty and that the tests represent a truncated development programme for the solid-fuelled missiles that gave way to the design tested from 1992 to 1996.

57 It is reported as a 400kt yield in Lewis and Xue, *China's Strategic Seapower*, p. 177, and as a 200–300kt yield in Lewis and Hua, 'China's Ballistic Missile Programs', *International Security*, p. 30. Both are cited according to general design plans.

58 This clustering is a composite of multiple interpretations of the available seismic data, as described in Jeffrey Lewis, *The Minimum Means of Reprisal*, p. 92. See Aoife O'Mongain, Alan Douglas and John B. Young, 'Body-wave Magnitudes and Locations of Presumed Explosions at the Chinese Test Site, 1967–1996', 22nd Annual DoD/DoE Seismic Research Symposium: Planning for Verification of and Compliance with the Comprehensive Nuclear Test-Ban Treaty, New Orleans, LA, 15 September 2000; John R. Murphy, 'Yield Estimation and Bias at the Chinese Lop Nor Test Site', 14th Annual DARPA/PL Seismic Research Symposium, Tucson, Arizona, 18 September 1992; Xiaoping Yang, Robert North, Carl Romney and Paul G. Richards, 'Worldwide Nuclear Explosions', Colombia University, http://www.ldeo.columbia. edu/~richards/my_papers/ WW_nuclear_tests_IASPEI_HB.pdf.

59 'Annual Report to Congress: Military and Security Developments Involving the People's Republic of China', US Department of Defense, 2010, p. 2, http://www.defense.gov/ pubs/pdfs/2010_cmpr_final.pdf.

60 Russian throw-weights are from START aggregate data.

61 Feiveson, Paine and von Hippel, 'A Low Threshold Test Ban is Feasible'.

62 No title, NAIC-1442-0629-97, 10 December 1996, as reproduced in Bill Gertz, *Betrayal* (Washington, DC: Regnery, 2001), pp. 251–52.

63 Alex Wellerstein, 'Kilotons per kilogram', *Restricted Data*, 23 December 2013, http://blog. nuclearsecrecy.com/2013/12/23/ kilotons-per-kilogram/.

64 Office of Scientific and Weapons Research, Central Intelligence Agency, *China's Nuclear Weapons*

Testing: Facing Prospects for a Comprehensive Ban, 30 September 1993, approved for release October 2003. Available at: http://www.foia.cia.gov/sites/default/files/document_conversions/89801/DOC_0000996367.pdf

65 Office of Scientific and Weapons Research, Central Intelligence Agency, *China's Nuclear Weapons Testing: Facing Prospects for a Comprehensive Ban*, 30 September 1993, approved for release October 2003. Available at: http://www.foia.cia.gov/sites/default/files/document_conversions/89801/DOC_0000996367.pdf; 'China Seeking Foreign Assistance To Address Concerns About Nuclear Stockpile Under CTBT', *Proliferation Digest*, 29 March 1996, p. 38. Available at: http://www.foia.cia.gov/sites/default/files/document_conversions/89801/DOC_0000996348.pdf

66 Senior Chinese official, 'The Modernization of Nuclear Weapon', 3rd Meeting of Sino-American Strategic Nuclear Relations and Strategic Bilateral Conference, 9–10 June 2008, Beijing.

67 For example, satellite images show the road leading to the site was recently resurfaced.

68 Jeffrey Lewis, 'Subcritical Testing at Lop Nor', Arms Control Wonk, 3 April 2009, http://lewis.armscontrolwonk.com/archive/2239/subcritical-testing-at-lop-nor.

69 Classified systems are probably better. In the mid-1990s in the US it was down to hundreds. By the end of the decade the IMS was better, probably comparable, but AEDS is probably better, albeit not that far

off. See: Jeffrey Lewis, 'AFTAC', Arms Control Wonk, 19 July 2011, http://lewis.armscontrolwonk.com/archive/4264/aftac. See also Ola Dahlam, Svein Mykkeltveit and Hein Haak, *Nuclear Test Ban: Converting Political Visions to Reality* (Stockholm: Springer, 2009).

70 Jeffrey Lewis, 'AFTAC', Arms Control Wonk, 19 July 2011, http://lewis.armscontrolwonk.com/archive/4264/aftac.

71 One estimate reports that 'tests with yields on the order of 100 tons would not be detected seismically [at Lop Nor], even if there were no attempt at evasion [such as decoupling]'. From 'Possible Future Activities at China's Nuclear Test Site,' *Proliferation Digest*, November 1996, p.23. Available at: http://www.foia.cia.gov/sites/default/files/document_conversions/89801/DOC_0000522904.pdf

72 A senior Chinese official has stated that China does not conduct so-called 'hydronuclear' tests that produce small amounts of yield that would evade detection. For current US estimates of monitoring capabilities, see National Research Council, *The Comprehensive Nuclear Test Ban Treaty: Technical Issues for the United States* (Washington DC: The National Academies Press, 2012).

73 US intelligence appears to have been primarily concerned with the computing power of the Galaxy-II computer. See 'China: The Galaxy-II Computer and Nuclear-Related Research', CIA, 3 August 1994, approved for release October 2003.

74 'China's Tianhe-2 Supercomputer Maintains Top Spot on 42nd TOP500 List', Top500, http://www.

top500.org/blog/lists/2013/11/ press-release/.

75 De Geer, 'The radioactive signature of the hydrogen bomb'.

76 Dan Stober and Ian Hoffman, *A Convenient Spy: Wen Ho Lee and the Politics of Nuclear Espionage* (New York: Simon & Schuster, 2007) p.233.

77 *Ibid.*, p.234.

78 *Ibid.*, 234

79 The Cox Report.

80 The concept of two-point implosion appeared in open literature as early as a 1956 drawing of a Swedish nuclear-weapons design that formed the basis of the Nth country experiment, in which two US graduate students designed a nuclear device based on open-source information.

81 David Wise, *Tiger Trap: America's Secret Spy War with China* (Boston: Houghton Mifflin Harcourt, 2011) pp.50–58.

82 Harold Agnew, 'Looking for Spies in the Nuclear Kitchen', Letter to the editor, *Wall Street Journal*, 17 May 1999, p. A27, http://www.fas. org/irp/ops/ci/agnewwsj.html.

83 *Ibid.*

CHAPTER THREE

China's fissile-material production

The availability of fissile material was from the outset a major factor shaping the pace and scope of Chinese nuclear-weapons deployments. Chinese weaponeers decided to pursue uranium implosion for their first nuclear test, an unusual choice for the time that reflected the relative state of the country's fissile material facilities.

Fissile-material production also created the major bureaucratic divide within China's strategic weapons programme, between the research and development bureaucracy that designed nuclear weapons and the defence-production bureaucracy that supplied fissile material. In the early years of China's strategic weapons programme, each competed for total control of the nuclear-weapons effort. Fissile material production was separated from the nuclear-weapons development programme. One Chinese expert recounts that he only discovered the location of China's fissile material production facilities when they appeared in the Western press. Before that, he only had a phone number.

The history of China's fissile material production is a matter of continuing interest. China appears to have stopped production of fissile material at the end of the 1980s as its nuclear-energy industry attempted to transform itself into a global industry. The end of fissile-material production seemed driven by the process of market reform more than by strategic calculation. As a result, China's historical production of fissile material may represent a constraint on the size of China's nuclear arsenal, at least in the near to medium term.

Historical narrative

China's fissile-material production complex reflects the legacy of Soviet assistance, as well as the decisions made in the wake of the withdrawal of Soviet advisers in 1960.

China's leaders initially expected to acquire a nuclear industry with substantial Soviet assistance. Over the course of the 1950s, China and the Soviet Union signed six agreements providing for Soviet assistance to the Chinese nuclear programme.[1] These agreements outlined Soviet assistance in constructing facilities for a small, albeit broad, nuclear programme including facilities to enrich uranium and to produce separated plutonium. One consequence was the decision to site a gaseous diffusion plant to enrich uranium near Lanzhou (Plant 504) and a plutonium production reactor and PUREX-type reprocessing plant near Yumen in Jiuquan prefecture (Plant 404), Gansu province.[2]

The decision to site the uranium-enrichment facility at Lanzhou, where an aviation plant was already under construction, was taken by Soviet and Chinese officials in late 1956. Approximately 200 Soviet experts arrived in May 1958 to design the enrichment plant, apparently using the Soviet enrichment plant at Novouralsk as a model. The Soviets agreed to supply the diffusion stages, which began arriving in January 1959, but refused Chinese personnel access to some of the equipment at the gaseous diffusion plant, prompting China to establish a diffusion laboratory in Beijing.[3]

The Soviet Union also agreed to supply China with a light-water graphite-moderated reactor and plutonium reprocessing plant, apparently similar to the 600-megawatt (MW) reactor at Tomsk. Construction of the plutonium-production reactor and reprocessing line near Jiuquan was much less advanced when Soviet advisers departed in 1960. The Chinese only managed to pour the foundation for the reactor and the Soviets did not deliver any sensitive equipment.[4]

The end of Soviet assistance prompted a debate within China's leadership about whether to continue a nuclear-weapons programme. China was recovering from the the catastrophe of the Great Leap Forward.

Ultimately, China's leaders chose to keep going, but with substantial modifications. China adopted a policy of 'contracting the front' – a military metaphor relating to concentrating forces on the most important tasks.[5] The gaseous diffusion plant near Lanzhou was deemed a first-line (or first-front) facility. A central feature of China's early period of fissile-material production was a decision to concentrate resources on producing a nuclear explosion by the end of 1964. As a result, China pursued uranium implosion for its early nuclear weapons.

Although the Soviets had not completed the Lanzhou plant, enough equipment was in place when Soviet advisers withdrew in August 1960 to allow China to complete the facility in about a year. The Chinese apparently chose to produce HEU in batches, refeeding enriched uranium into the upper stages of the cascade, to meet the leadership's end-of-1964 deadline for the first nuclear test.

The plutonium-production reactor and reprocessing line were designated 'second-line' (or second-front) facilities. China would not complete the plutonium-production reactor at Jiuquan until 1966 and the reprocessing facility would not begin operation until 1970. Many conventional armaments programmes were also delayed.

The US intelligence community largely missed this reorientation of China's fissile-material production. It incorrectly interpreted the slowdown in production of conventional armaments as evidence of a broader retrenchment following the disastrous Great Leap Forward and the withdrawal of Soviet assistance.

Chinese accounts record near-heroic efforts by Chinese workers to bring the plant into operation in time to meet the 1964 deadline for China's first nuclear test. The US intelligence community, by contrast, incorrectly believed that the Lanzhou gaseous diffusion plant remained under construction during this period and was, in any event, too small to produce HEU.

China's October 1964 nuclear test surprised US officials who had expected that China's first nuclear weapon would use plutonium. In the wake of the test, the US intelligence community posited that a third country, such as the Soviet Union or France, had supplied China with its HEU. Analysts then proceeded to argue that China must have used another facility, such as an electromagnetic isotope separation facility, to 'top off' the enriched uranium to weapons grade. During this period, the US also misidentified a fuel-fabrication plant near Baotou as a plutonium-production reactor.

In 1965, China began constructing 'third-front' (or third-line) facilities to replicate the first- and second-front facilities built with Soviet assistance.[6] China's leaders placed third-front facilities inland, largely in Sichuan province, far away from both China's coast and the Soviet border. Although the third-front facilities improved in some ways on China's first generation of fissile-material production facilities, the overall effort was driven by the same ideological concerns as the Cultural Revolution. Third-front projects were often marked by poor planning and unrealistic objectives.

In most cases, China shifted the location of both third-front fissile-material production facilities from the initial sites selected in Sichuan. The initial replacement site for the Lanzhou gaseous diffusion plant was moved almost immediately after Chinese officials determined that the site was too far from the river that could supply the water necessary to cool the plant. In November 1965, Deng Xiaoping and Bo Yibo made a site inspection near Jinkouhe (alternative name Heping), where China eventually built the third-front gaseous diffusion plant.[7] The Jinkouhe facility (Plant 814) became operational in 1970.[8]

China continued work for several years at another site, an underground plutonium-production reactor and reprocessing line near Fuling (Plant 816) intended to replace the Jiuquan reactor.[9] This project experienced numerous delays. By 1969, Chinese leaders had determined these delays were unacceptable given the possibility of war with the Soviet Union. They initiated a new series of projects called the '820 projects'.[10] In terms of fissile-material production, the most important 820 project was an above-ground plutonium production reactor and reprocessing facility near Guangyuan (Plant 821) that ultimately replaced Jiuquan.[11]

At first glance, the decision to begin construction of an above-ground reactor appears to represent a triumph of pragmatism. However, the story of the 820 projects is more complicated, as one would expect given the chaos of the Cultural Revolution. Other 820 projects include a massive underground bunker for Lin Biao and two other, previously undisclosed, underground nuclear reactors that were never completed. Construction crews from Fuling were moved to Yichang to begin constructing a reactor using CANada Deuterium Uranium (CANDU) technology, which is very different from the design of reactors at Jiuquan, Fuling and Guangyuan.[12] China also began research and excavation at a site intended to host an underground fast-breeder reactor near Changping, in the outer suburbs of Beijing.[13]

With the deaths of Zhou Enlai and Mao Zedong in 1976, China entered a new period. The Cultural Revolution came to an end. Deng Xiaoping and a number of veteran revolutionaries, later referred to as 'the Elders', gradually marginalised Mao's chosen successor, Hua Guofeng. Although remembered as a reformer, Deng's relaxation of Maoist policies occurred

China's underground reactors

During the Cultural Revolution, China began construction of several never-completed underground nuclear reactors. The best known is the 816 Plant near Fuling. Two additional underground reactors – a CANada Deuterium Uranium (CANDU)-type reactor near Yichang and a fast-breeder reactor on the outskirts of Beijing – have not previously been described in any English-language account. These efforts were part of the construction of third-line industrial facilities, with Fuling beginning in 1965, while construction at Yichang (as well as the above-ground reactor near Guangyuan) began during the 1969 Sino-Soviet crisis. These projects suffered from the same unrealistic leadership expectations and poor planning that hampered other third-line industrial projects in the late 1960s and 1970s. On balance, the experience of China's underground nuclear reactors tends to suggest that Chinese efforts to build additional facilities to produce fissile material were unsuccessful.

China began constructing the underground 816 Plant near Fuling in 1965 as part of the third-line effort to relocate industries inland. The effort was vastly inefficient. The 816 reactor was planned to serve as a replacement for the plutonium-production reactor at Jiuquan. The slow progress at Fuling led China's leaders to begin construction on the above-ground reactor near Guangyuan, which became China's third-line plutonium production facility. Construction continued slowly at Fuling, although China abandoned the project in 1980 before completion. The site was declassified in 2003 and opened to Chinese tourists a few years later.

In 1969, China began building three new reactors as part of a second wave of third-line facilities, referred to as the 820 projects. The most well-known of these was Lin Biao's command bunker, which is now open to tourists. Meanwhile, China began construction of an above-ground gradually and only with the consensus of other elders.

A major feature of Deng Xiaoping's early economic policies was conversion of defence industries to civil use. Nuclear facilities were not exempt from this process.[14] This shift resulted in a reduction and eventual cessation of China's production of fissile material for weapons purposes, apparently without serious consideration of the possibility that China's fissile material needs might change.

reactor near Guangyuan (Plant 821) and a second underground reactor near Yichang (Plant 827). The former was apparently intended as a stop-gap measure until Fuling and other underground reactors could be completed. In July 1969, Lin reportedly ordered the reactor pile at Jiuquan relocated, before technical personnel persuaded Zhou Enlai that this was impossible.[15]

Plant 827 was a CANDU-type heavy-water reactor. Chinese sources indicate that the reactor was never completed. One structure appears to be a pump house along the river to provide a secondary cooling loop for the reactor.

China also attempted to build a breeder reactor in the outer suburbs of Beijing, at the site of today's Institute for Nuclear and Energy Technology (INET) near Changping, affiliated with Tsinghua University. Despite fast-breeder reactors being vastly more complicated technological undertakings than traditional reactors, Chinese leaders set the impossible goal of transmitting power into Tiananmen Square by October 1970. Engineers began excavation work in the hills north of INET for the breeder reactor, but it did not seem that any equipment was installed. INET ceased work on the breeder reactor by 1979.

Although the presence of the underground reactor at Fuling is sometimes used to suggest China may operate a large number of unknown underground reactors, the history of the three underground reactor projects demonstrates how the leadership turmoil and unrealistic planning of the late 1960s slowed China's efforts to produce fissile material. These underground reactors were expensive failures that China abandoned following Mao's death and Deng Xiaoping's consolidation of power. If the question is why China constructed so few facilities to produce plutonium for the weapons programme, part of the answer is that it started several but ultimately only completed a few.

China's decision to convert and ultimately shut down its fissile-material production facilities represented a shift in philosophy rather than a strategic decision. Zhou Enlai had said the nuclear industry should be more than a 'Ministry of Explosions'. Initially, under Nie Rongzhen, China invested in defence technologies with the expectation that such investments would 'spin off' and lift the civil scientific, technological and industrial bases. By the late 1970s, it was clear to many Chinese leaders that the defence bureaucracy was woefully inefficient and unable to produce benefits for the civilian economy. Perhaps worst of all, the dreadful performance of the PLA in the 1979 campaign against Vietnam suggested the defence bureaucracy failed to produce even decent arms. Over the course of the 1980s, China's leaders dramatically reduced defence spending, attempting to convert moribund defence enterprises to passable civilian firms. This process was particularly hard for the nuclear industry. Ultimately what would become the China National Nuclear Corporation concluded that China's existing base of defence technologies for fissile-material production was too inefficient and expensive to support a civilian energy programme.

During the 1980s, China developed and constructed its first domestic nuclear power plant, Qinshan 1, which it connected to the electricity grid in 1991. China rationalised its fissile-material production facilities, initially converting the first generation of these to civilian use, then decommissioning them. At the same time, unrealistic projects to place nuclear reactors underground at Fuling, Yichang and Changping were stopped.

By about 1980, China appears to have ended production of HEU at the Lanzhou gaseous diffusion plant, converting the plant to the production of low-enriched uranium (LEU). China decommissioned the Lanzhou plant in the late 1990s. It began converting the Jiuquan reactor to civil power production in 1984 and decommissioned it by the end of the 1980s.[16]

China subsequently converted its third-line facilities. Chinese officials have privately said that by 1987 all enrichment capacity was producing LEU for civil use.[17] Other Chinese sources stated that China 'stopped producing plutonium for weapons purposes in 1991'.[18] These dates probably reflect the civilian conversion of the enrichment facility at Jinkouhe and the nuclear reactor at Guangyuan.

Despite a process of defense conversion that appears to have ended the production of fissile material, the Chinese government has not publicly declared a moratorium. Still, officials privately suggest that China is not producing HEU or plutonium for weapons purposes. As recently as February 2005, Chinese officials told a visiting Australian official that he 'should infer from [Chinese support for a treaty banning fissile-material production] that China was not producing such fissile-material'.[19] The Chinese reluctance to articulate a public moratorium may reflect the fact that fissile-material production ended without a specific strategic rationale. Chinese officials may also wish to protect information regarding the historical production of HEU, the status of certain facilities and the continuing secrecy around facilities such as the failed effort to build a CANDU reactor near Yichang.

During the 1990s, China began seeking commercially viable enrichment and reprocessing technologies to support a civil nuclear fuel cycle. The technologies developed for the weapons programme were inefficient and not suitable for large-scale commercial operation.

In particular, China sought to replace its gaseous diffusion plants for uranium enrichment with centrifuge plants. China has long had a centrifuge research programme, located near Hanzhong.[20] In the 1990s, China began purchasing enrichment services and centrifuge plants from Russia for civilian production. China has announced plans to develop domestic centrifuge plants with enough capacity to supply domestic demand, which is predicted to top 7 million separative work units (SWU) per year by 2020. (The 'separative work unit' or SWU is the standard measure of the capacity to separate uranium isotopes.) China is now building indigenous centrifuge facilities, believed to use technology similar to that imported from Russia.

Today, China also has an ambitious nuclear-energy plan that calls for 150 gigawatts (electric) of installed capacity by 2030 and, eventually, the development of a closed fuel cycle.[21] With regard to the latter, it has built a prototype fast reactor near Beijing and a pilot reprocessing facility near Jiuquan. It's negotiating with French multinational group AREVA over the construction of a reprocessing facility and a mixed oxide fuel (MOX) fabrication plant in Jiuquan.

Although these facilities are not believed to be directly involved in defence production, the China National Nuclear Corporation (CNNC) retains a national defence mission and could, if directed, construct facilities to restart fissile-material production.

Estimating fissile-material production

How much plutonium and HEU has China produced? China has not declared its fissile-material production, as the US and Russia have done. There are a number of open-source estimates making use of declassified US intelligence estimates, Chinese materials and contemporary reporting. These estimates are shown in Table 2. The current best estimate, calculated by David Albright using a sampling method and based in part on information presented in this chapter for the first time, is that China produced between 13 and 26 tonnes of HEU and 1.6–2.4 tonnes of plutonium. The median production estimates are 19 tonnes of HEU and 1.9 tonnes of plutonium.

Table 2: **Existing Estimates of Chinese Fissile Material Production for Weapons Purposes**

	HEU Production (t)	Military Plutonium Production (t)
Albright (2014)	13–26	1.6–2.4
Past Estimates		
US Department of Energy (1999)		1.7–2.8
Albright et al. (1996)	15–25	2–6
Albright and Hinderstein (2005)	17–26	2.3–3.2
Zhang (2011)	12–20	1.5–2.5

The 2014 estimate from Albright is from a forthcoming revision of Albright and Hinderstein, *Global Stocks of Nuclear Explosive Material* – End 2003 (Institute for Science and International Security, Updated 2005), funded by the Nuclear Threat Initiative. The estimate for China is based, in part, on new information about China's fissile-material production presented in this chapter for the first time. Other Sources are: Robert S. Norris and William M. Arkin, 'World Plutonium Inventories – 1999', Natural Resources Defense Council, from the *Bulletin of the Atomic Scientists*, September/October 1999; David Albright, Frans Berkhout and William Walker, 'World Inventory of Plutonium and Highly Enriched Uranium 1996; World Inventories, Capabilities and Policies', SIPRI (Oxford: Oxford University Press, 1997); David Albright and Corey Hinderstein, 'Chinese Military Plutonium and Highly Enriched Uranium Inventories', 30 June 2005, http://isis-online.org/uploads/isis-reports/documents/chinese_military_inventories.pdf; and Zhang Hui, 'China's Fissile Material Production and Stocks', in *Global Fissile Material Report 2010: Balancing the Books* (Princeton, NJ: Princeton University Press, 2011).

Despite differences in methodology and underlying data, the open-source estimates are generally consistent with one another, even if the reported ranges can be quite large and sensitive to differences in assumptions and methods. As David Albright, Frans Berkhout and William Walker noted in their seminal 1996 study, they are marked by a 'high degree of uncertainty'.[22]

In general, the normal method to estimate Chinese fissile-material production is to use declassified US intelligence estimates as a baseline, incorporate details about the operational history of the facilities based on authoritative Chinese sources, then use contemporary reporting to triangulate estimates of the capacity and operational history of each facility.

The limitations in data are significant. Early US estimates were often incorrect in terms of both capacity and operational status, while reports of the contemporary capacity of facilities can vary considerably. Moreover, many contemporary reports are necessarily based on conversations with Chinese officials who may be mistaken or misunderstood.

Fortunately, as China's period of fissile-material production recedes into the past, more information is becoming available. Individuals who worked at various plants have begun to publish memoirs, often online. Two Chinese-language reminiscences, for example, provide crucial details about China's plutonium-production complex. Zheng Jingdong, a former engineer at Guangyuan, published numerous entries on his blog concerning his work and his perspective on the decision to establish Guangyuan. He details the construction of the facility, technical issues plant workers experienced and Guangyuan's conversion to civilian use.[23] Cui Zhaohui, a retired physicist who worked at Jiuquan and the Institute for Nuclear Energy Technology, sheds further light on activities at Jiuquan and other previously undisclosed sites.

China's HEU facilities

China produced HEU for its weapons programme at two facilities: the Lanzhou Gaseous Diffusion Plant (Plant 504), from 1963 to 1980; and the Jinkouhe Gaseous Diffusion Plant (Plant 814), from 1970 to 1987.

Early US estimates regarding the Lanzhou plant were wildly incorrect. They believed the plant was not operational at the time of China's first nuclear explosion in October 1964 and, in any event, too small to produce HEU.

The US made a series of errors, including incorrectly measuring the size of the main building and ignoring smaller connected buildings that may have contained diffusion stages. China also initially used batch production, an inefficient process discounted by the US intelligence community.

Finally, US estimates appear to also have been hampered by a lack of understanding about improvements at comparable Soviet facilities. The Soviet Union supplied much of the equipment in the Lanzhou plant, possibly using equipment taken from the decommissioned D1 plant at Novouralsk. They did not, however, provide the gaseous diffusion barriers, which the Chinese developed themselves.

The Soviet D1 plant held approximately 7,000 diffusion stages. The Lanzhou gaseous diffusion plant was somewhat smaller, but could probably accommodate at least 6,000 Soviet-style diffusion stages. The D1 plant was capable of producing tens of kilogrammes of HEU per year or about 10 tonnes of separative work.

China gradually increased capacity at Lanzhou. In the mid-1970s, the CIA estimated the output of the Lanzhou plant as between 30 and 60 metric tonnes of SWU annually. *China Today* states it increased the capacity of Lanzhou 'many fold' by 1985 and the efficiency of the plant 'approximated international levels'.[24] Given the physical size of the Lanzhou facility when compared to contemporary facilities in the Soviet Union (1955–1957) and France (1960), the Lanzhou gaseous diffusion plant may have had a capacity of 160–200 tonnes of SWU per year by the mid-1980s.[25] In 1997, Mark Hibbs subsequently reported that the Lanzhou plant had a 'nominal throughput' of 180 tonnes of SWU per year.[26]

China stopped producing HEU at Lanzhou sometime in the 1980s, possibly as early as 1980. A Chinese reporter who visited the site in 1984 noted that the process of defence conversion had begun some years earlier.

There are other higher estimates, particularly from industry sources. In some cases, these may reflect estimates derived from China's demand for enrichment services or the assumption that all China's enrichment work was performed at Lanzhou.[27] It is also possible that China may have further increased the capacity of Lanzhou during its period of civil LEU production.

China decommissioned the gaseous diffusion plant at Lanzhou around 1998. Currently it has constructed a Russian centrifuge plant and the first of several plants using indigenous centrifuges to supply the country's civil demand for LEU.

The third-line gaseous diffusion plant near Jinkouhe began operations in 1970, some five years after construction started.[28] As with Lanzhou, the US intelligence community failed to recognise when Jinkouhe became operational: a 1972 assessment concluded that the plant had not yet begun operations.

The physical layout of the plant near Jinkouhe differs from that at Lanzhou, as it appears to comprise two large cascade halls connected with partially underground piping.[29]

If China uses both buildings to enrich uranium, which is the configuration the US expected to see at Lanzhou, estimates of floor space would suggest a total maximum capacity of 350–450 tonnes of SWU. According to a Chinese official, Jinkouhe is only 'a little larger' than the facility at Lanzhou. It's possible that a different layout reflects a less dense configuration of diffusion stages, possibly for superior temperature control, which was a major reason for re-siting the plant.[30] If one conservatively assumes that Jinkouhe has 50% more capacity than Lanzhou, the total peak production would be 240–300 tonnes of SWU. Other estimates place the capacity at 200–250 tonnes of SWU per year.

The plant probably stopped producing HEU in 1987. Radiation dose estimates of workers suggest the plant continued enriching uranium through 2003, while thermal images from 2013 confirm the enrichment halls remain much warmer than surrounding buildings. According to a paper on dose estimates at Jinkouhe, the lower doses starting in the mid-1990s reflect layoffs that reduced the operating capacity of the plant.[31]

Plutonium

The best open-source estimates place China's production of plutonium between 1.6 and 2.4 metric tonnes, with a median of 1.9 metric tonnes. A leaked Department of Energy estimate places China's total production at 1.7–2.8 metric tonnes of plutonium. China produced plutonium for its weapons programme at two facilities: the Jiuquan Integrated Atomic Energy Enterprise (Plant 404) from 1966 to 1984 and Guangyuan (Plant 821) from 1975 to 1991.

The Soviet Union provided relatively little assistance for China's plutonium-production reactor and reprocessing line. China completed development of a light-water-cooled, graphite-moderated reactor in 1966. China also established a Plutonium Uranium Extraction Plant (PUREX) reprocessing line, starting with an interim plant, followed by a military facility.

The reactor appeared to have a design capacity of 600MW, which is consistent with upper-bound estimates based on cooling towers.[32] The reactor almost certainly never operated at this capacity for any sustained period. Cui Zhaohui, a retired engineer who worked at the plant, describes a serious accident at the reactor in 1969, reports frequent problems with the fuel rods after a few years of operation that 'seriously affected the production capacity of the reactor' and describes a 100-day shutdown to repair leaking pipes. This account suggests the reactor suffered serious operational disruptions through the mid-1970s, after which Cui was posted to Beijing.[33] Existing estimates of the average power of the reactor during its lifetime vary. Few outside experts believe it exceeded 400MW at any point. The relatively low estimate of 1.7–2.8 tonnes, attributed to the US Department of Energy, may reflect these concerns.

China began to convert Jiuquan to electricity production in 1984, although it's unclear if this process was completed. The reactor was shut down by the end of the 1980s. Satellite photographs from the mid-2000s show yellow barrels for radioactive waste at the site, suggesting that decommissioning was well under way by that time. Like Lanzhou, China has converted the Jiuquan Atomic Energy Complex to civil nuclear-energy uses. Today Jiuquan is the site of China's pilot civil reprocessing facility. China is currently negotiating the purchase of an industrial-scale reprocessing and MOX fabrication plant from the French firm AREVA, which is expected to be located at Jiuquan.

Relatively little is known about the capacity of the reactor at Guangyuan and its reprocessing facility. One of the few sources is the account of a former engineer, Zheng Jingdong, who claims to have worked there. Zheng explains that the reactor and reprocessing line were duplicates of the facilities at Jiuquan in terms of 'principles and process', but differed in other ways that imply a higher capacity to produce and separate plutonium.

According to Zheng, the project began in April 1969 as a 'rush build' that was part of Lin Biao's 'war preparations' campaign.[34] The campaign would precede the Autumn evacuation of Beijing during the Sino-Soviet crisis. The reactor went critical in 1973.

Zheng mentions three periods of being operational: efforts from 1973 to 1976 to bring the reactor and reprocessing line into full operation; efforts from 1977 to 1980 to improve the efficiency of the reactor and the reprocessing; and efforts from 1981 to 1986 to extend the life of the reactor and reprocessing line. Some accounts suggest the reactor stopped producing plutonium for weapons purposes in 1987. In 1990, it became an aluminium production facility.

The reactor at Guangyuan also suffered operational problems, according to Zheng, but these seem less serious than those reported at Jiuquan. They related to the cooling system, particularly large pumps, as well as the piping that carried water to the heat exchanger.

Conclusion

US estimates of China's production of fissile material were generally good. The numbers are not precise, but are sufficient to exclude the most extreme estimates of the Chinese production of HEU and plutonium. New information has not resulted in dramatic changes to past estimates. In general, the trend has been towards revising down production estimates as analysts better understand the less-than-perfect operational histories of the facilities. This is unsurprising, as one would expect initial estimates to represent a sort of worst-case scenario.

The current best estimate of the total stockpile of plutonium and HEU, including material in current warheads, is 1.9 tonnes of plutonium and 19 tonnes of HEU. Chinese warheads are believed to use plutonium in their primaries, with HEU for secondaries. The total stockpile is sufficient for a few hundred such warheads – and no more than several hundred at the most.[35] This is broadly consistent with leaked US estimates that China produced between 1.7 and 2.8 tonnes of plutonium, as well as estimates that China's stockpile of fissile material was sufficient for planned modernisation.

This production estimate is also consistent with declassified US estimates placing the number of Chinese nuclear weapons between 200 and 300.[36] Given limited fissile-material holdings, the arsenal cannot be as high as the 1,800 estimate asserted by a former Russian chief of staff and nowhere near the 3,000 number claimed by a 2011 study from Georgetown University students.[37]

It seems unlikely at this point that there are additional facilities producing significant quantities of fissile material. The flood of information about formerly secret projects is impressive, from first-person accounts to sensitive information that shows up online in curricula vitae and scholarship awards. Fuling, Yichang and Changping escaped notice in part because they never went into operation. There may yet be surprises to come, but the enthusiasm for underground reactors appears to have been a phenomenon specific to the madness of the Cultural Revolution.

At the same time, China is far more transparent today. While Chinese officials do not acknowledge the gaseous diffusion plant at Jinkouhe and the district remains closed to foreigners, a corruption scandal concerning the director in 2011 was widely documented online. A local government website details appearances by the disgraced director and by his successor, as well as visit by a CNNC official. Local newspapers have published the allegations against the former director, including photographs of related court documents. When local officials arranged a field trip for the management of the plant to a local prison, presumably to remind them of the consequences of corruption, this visit was reported in the press as well. This is to say nothing of technical papers relating to the doses received by workers, or the many photographs and accounts of Chinese tourists who have visited the area.

Historical intelligence estimates hold up relatively well, particularly considering the lack of insight into the politics that drove many decisions in the late 1960s. Still, there were significant mistakes. The US missed China's decision to go it alone in 1961 and did not anticipate that economic reform would end fissile-material production. The US intelligence community also did well in identifying sites under construction, although they tended to make mistakes about the purpose, capacity or status of sites. It has long been believed that 'US intelligence identified all of China's major NEM [nuclear explosive materials] production facilities prior to their operation'.[38] New evidence suggests that Jinkouhe was a very close call, if it was in fact detected prior to beginning production. Jinkouhe was a hard target, given its location (fog-shrouded mountain gorges) and the relatively limited technology at the time. Analysts were also hampered by a tendency to assume Chinese decisions would be strategic and mirror their own. There may be lessons in this experience for assessing the intentions and capabilities of today's nuclear aspirants.

Perhaps the most important insight relates to the subject of fissile-material constraints and the Fissile Material Cut-off Treaty (FMCT). China appears to have stopped fissile-material production and retired facilities, without replacing them. Although China's civil facilities demonstrate an ability to restart fissile-material production, the transformation of the nuclear complex to civilian energy is breathtaking. In particular, China has completely abandoned the generation of technologies that produced the country's weapons programmes, having deemed the technologies used for military production inadequate for a civilian programme. China has emphasised importing foreign enrichment and reprocessing technologies as part of a comprehensive, closed fuel cycle.

As a result, China may be fissile-material constrained. The country's stockpile of plutonium may limit arsenal size based on the designs deployed and tested before 1996. China could, of course, attempt to reorient existing civil facilities, but it is clear that the CNNC is now focused on becoming a global energy company. It has taken Zhou Enlai's admonition to be more than a 'Ministry of Explosions' far beyond what anyone might have expected in the 1980s. CNNC maintains a national defence mission, though it seems that mission is to maintain a capacity to restart production if needed.

Notes

[1] See John Lewis and Xue Litai, *China Builds the Bomb* (Stanford University Press, 1988), p. 62

[2] Jiuquan is a prefectural-level municipality covering more than 190,000 square kilometres. Both the Jiquan Atomic Energy Complex and the Jiquan Space Launch Center are located within the large area of Jiquan prefecture, albeit separated by about 200km. The US intelligence community has historically referred to these facilities by the nearest populated place, Yumen and Shuangchengzi.

[3] Lewis and Xue, *China Builds the Bomb*, p. 118.

[4] *Ibid.*, pp. 113–14

[5] *China Today: Defense Science and Technology* (Beijing, National

Defense University Press, 1993) pp. 41–59.

6 Ibid., pp. 58–59. See also Barry Naughton, 'The Third Front: Defence Industrialization in the Chinese Interior', China Quarterly, no. 115, September 1988, pp. 351–86.

7 Heping is a small Yi-nationality village in the Jinkouhe District. The US initially referred to this facility as 'Chingkouho'. On the Deng and Bo visit, see China Today, Nuclear Industry, JPRS-CST-88-002, 15 January 1988, p. 6.

8 A timeline provided by the China Nuclear Energy Association (CNEA) lists this date. See China Nuclear Energy Association, China Nuclear Energy, 2009, 编者注, available at: http://www.china-nea.cn/html/2009-11/4239.html; direct translation of the original entry: 'June 25, 1970: 814 Plant is completed and put into operation to achieve products meeting required standards.'

9 On the revelation of Fuling, see http://www2.gwu.edu/~nsarchiv/NSAEBB/NSAEBB372/docs/Underground-Clips.pdf.

10 '820' may refer to the 20 August 1968 Soviet invasion of Czechoslovakia.

11 See the timeline provided by CNEA at http://www.china-nea.cn/html/2009-11/4239.html.

12 China also attempted to build an underground fast-breeder reactor near Beijing. Construction probably did not progress beyond tunnelling.

13 A history of Tsinghua University provides details. See http://www.tsinghua.edu.cn/publish/inet/3578/.

14 China Today, p. 58.

15 http://qxzc.net/gr/cuizh/4/4(8).htm.

16 China Today, Nuclear Industry, JPRS-CST-88-002, 15 January 1988, p.24.

17 Ann MacLachlan and Mark Hibbs, 'China Stops Production of Military Fuel: All SWU Capacity Now for Civil Use', Nuclear Fuel, vol. 14, no. 23, 13 November 1989. Albright and Hinderstein subsequently quote Hibbs stating that the cut-off was in 1987.

18 Robert S. Norris, Andrew S. Burrows and Richard W. Fieldhouse, 'Nuclear Weapons Databook: British, French, and Chinese Nuclear Weapons', Volume V (Boulder, CO: Natural Resources Defense Council, 1994), p. 350.

19 In March 2004, John Carlson, then director-general of the Australian Safeguards and Nonproliferation Office, briefed US embassy officials on his 19–24 February trip to Beijing to begin talks on Australian uranium sales to China. William Stanton, then DCM in Canberra, summarised Carlson's briefing in a cable subsequently released by Wikileaks. See 'Discussions begin for China to buy Australian Uranium', 4 March 2005, http://www.wikileaks.org/plusd/cables/05CANBERRA432_a.html.

20 A.Q. Khan claims to have helped China construct a centrifuge plant at this location, in exchange for Chinese assistance to Pakistan's programme including 50kg of HEU. It's difficult to assess the veracity of Khan's claims, although CNNC subsequently located some of the modules at Lanzhou to maintain the local workforce.

21 David Albright, Frans Berkhout and William Walker, 'World Inventory

of Plutonium and Highly Enriched Uranium 1996; World Inventories, Capabilities and Policies', SIPRI (Oxford: Oxford University Press, 1997).

22 See Zheng Jingdong's blog at http://blog.163.com/zjd_8213701/blog/static/33582026201171991110947.

23 *China Today*, Nuclear Industry, JPRS-CST-88-002, 15 January 1988, p. 15.

24 The Soviet D-5 building at Novouralsk, which began operating over 1955–57, was 13 hectares with a given capacity of 650t SWU per year or about 40t SWU per year per hectare. The French Pierlatte was 12 hectares with a given capacity of 500t SWU per year or 50t SWU per year per hectare. The gaseous diffusion plant at Lanzhou is about 3.9 hectares. Such a method cannot be used to accurately estimate the capacity of gaseous diffusion plants, which may vary in terms of the flow rate, cascade configuration and barrier design. Nonetheless, physical size offers a rough approximation of capacity that can be used with electricity consumption and other information to provide a rough estimate.

25 Mark Hibbs, 'With More Russian Centrifuges, China will Close Lanzhou Plant', *Nuclear Fuel,* vol. 22, no. 20, 6 October 1997. In 1989 Hibbs and MacLachlan quoted a 'knowledgeable industry source' stating that the throughput of the plant was 300t SWU per year. This number appears too high in light of the floorspace of the facility. Machlachlan and Hibbs, 'China Stops Production of Military HEU; All SWU Capacity Now for Civil Use', p. 5.

26 Until the early 1990s, most nuclear-industry experts assumed the most important, if not only, uranium-enrichment centre in China was at Lanzhou. Most people in the commercial sector did not know China had a gaseous diffusion plant at Jinkouhe, or, if they did know, assumed it was smaller than Lanzhou. It is possible that conclusions made on the basis of China's demand assumed that Lanzhou accounted for most, or even all, of Chinese gaseous diffusion capability.

27 Previous estimates have stated that the facility began operating in the mid-1970s, based on a 1972 DIA assessment that stated the facility was not yet operational. Data on annual radiation dose for workers at the plant confirms it began operating in 1970. See National Intelligence Estimate, China's Strategic Attack Programs, NIE 13-8-74, 13 June 1974, declassified version.

28 This was the configuration – a pair of large enrichment halls – that the US intelligence analysts expected to see at Lanzhou, which in part led to estimates that the facility was not yet operational.

29 An historical account notes that 'At that time, those in charge of siting the new uranium enrichment plant had different views. The original site had a scattered layout and the water temperature was such that a new site for construction should be considered.' See *Memories of Deng Xiaoping* (Beijing, Central Literature Publishing House, February 1998). Excerpt republished at: http://news.xinhuanet.

com/newscenter/2003-08/19/content_1034042.htm.

30 Wang Chengjian and Wang Dejin, 'Data Analysis and Evaluation of the Measurement of Occupational Exposure of Radioactive Materials in Plant 814', National Dose Monitoring and Evaluation Symposium, 2004, http://cpfd.cnki.com.cn/Article/CPFDTOTAL-EGVD200409001032.htm.

31 See Cui's memoir, available at: http://qxzc.net/gr/cuizh/4/4(2).htm.

32 Ibid.

33 See Zheng's blog, available at: http://blog.163.com/zjd_8213701/blog/static/33582026201171991110947.

34 China has, of course, expended some of the fissile material in its 45 nuclear-weapons tests. The simplest approach is to treat each of the 38 tests that used plutonium (CHIC-8–CHIC-45) as a single warhead expended. If one were to use the same 4–6kg range hypothesised for the average amount of plutonium in each warhead, that would suggest China consumed approximately 140–230kg of plutonium in nuclear tests. See also Zhang Hui, 'China's Fissile Material Production and Stocks', in Global Fissile Material Report 2010: Balancing the Books (Princeton, NJ: Princeton University Press, 2011).

35 For a declassified US assessment of China's stockpile, see 'China's Nuclear Weapons Testing: Facing Prospects for a Comprehensive Test Ban', CIA, Office of Scientific and Weapons Research, 30 September 1993; and 'China Seeking Foreign Assistance to Address Concerns about Nuclear Stockpile under CTBT', Proliferation Digest, 29 March 1996.

36 Viktor Yesin, 'China's Nuclear Capabilities', in Aleksey Arbatov, Vladimir Dvorkin and Sergey Oznobishchev (eds), Prospects of China's Participation in Nuclear Arms Limitation (Moscow: Institute of World Economic and International Relations, Russian Academy of Sciences, 2012). Translation available at: http://www.asianarmscontrol.org/content/prospects-chinas-participation-nuclear-arms-limitation. Philip A. Karber, 'Strategic Implications of China's Underground Great Wall', 26 September 2011, http://www.fas.org/nuke/guide/china/Karber_UndergroundFacilities-Full_2011_reduced.pdf.

37 Monitoring Nuclear Weapons and Nuclear Explosive Materials: An Assessment of Methods and Capabilities (Washington, DC: National Academies, 2005) p. 209.

CHAPTER FOUR

China's Missile Forces

Since 1964, China has relied on a nuclear deterrent of land-based ballistic missiles deployed with the Second Artillery Corps, a rough equivalent to Russia's Strategic Rocket Forces. No air-force units are believed to have a primary nuclear mission and China's new generation of ballistic-missile submarines (SSBN) is not yet operational. China is also deploying a variety of new short-range ballistic missiles, as well as ground- and air-launched cruise missiles, but these appear conventionally armed.

From the late 1950s, China sought to develop long-range ballistic missiles to deliver a planned arsenal of multi-mega-tonne fusion warheads. The 1958 Guidance on the Development of Nuclear Weapons emphasised thermonuclear weapons and long-range ballistic missiles, twin goals described as 'sophisticated weapons'.[1] Nevertheless, China did not deploy a significant number of nuclear-armed ballistic missiles until the mid-1970s, and did not deploy either the DF-4 or DF-5 ICBM in any significant number until the late 1980s.

Today, according to the Office of the Secretary of Defense's annual report to Congress on military and security developments, China deploys approximately 50–75 nuclear-armed ICBMs, as well as a force of nuclear-armed intermediate- and medium-range ballistic missiles:

> China's nuclear arsenal currently consists of approximately 50–75 ICBMs, including the silo-based CSS-4 (DF-5); the solid-fueled, road-mobile CSS-10 Mods 1 and 2 (DF-31 and DF-31A); and the more limited range CSS-3 (DF-4). This force is complemented by liquid-fueled CSS-2 intermediate-range ballistic missiles and road-mobile, solid-fueled CSS-5 (DF-21) MRBMs for regional deterrence missions. By 2015, China's nuclear forces will include additional CSS-10 Mod 2 and enhanced CSS-4 ICBMs.[2]

This description is consistent with the remarks of General Jing Zhiyuan, former commander of the Second Artillery, who told a US Congressional delegation in August 2007 that the Second Artillery's nuclear forces included 'the DF-3, DF-4, DF-5, DF-21, and DF-31 missiles on mobile platforms or silos'.[3] He described other missiles, such as the DF-11 and DF-15, as conventional.

Table 3. **China's Nuclear-Armed Ballistic Missiles**

Missile	US	Fuel	Deployment Mode	Range	Launchers
DF-3	CSS-2	Liquid	Transportable	3,000+	5–10
DF-4	CSS-3	Liquid	Rollout-to-launch	5,500+	10–15
DF-5A	CSS-4 Mod 2	Liquid	Silo	12,000+	About 20
DF-21/21A	CSS-5 Mods 1 and 2	Solid	Road-mobile	1,750+	Fewer than 50
DF-31	CSS-10 Mod 1	Solid	Road-mobile	7,000+	5–10
DF-31A	CSS-10 Mod 2	Solid	Road-mobile	11,000+	More than 15
Total					~110

National Air and Space Intelligence Center, Ballistic and Cruise Missile Threat, 2013. Available at: http://www.afisr.af.mil/shared/media/document/AFD-130710-054.pdf

Developing ballistic missiles

China's initial plans for developing an arsenal of ballistic missiles were unrealistic, mirroring the unrealistic planning of the Great Leap Forward era. In addition to a missile designated 1059 – a copy of a Soviet SS-2 that China planned to test by the October 1959 tenth anniversary of the founding of the PRC – China planned three missiles in the *Dongfeng* (or East Wind) series: the DF-1, DF-2 and DF-3. These missiles do not correspond to the ones that today bear these designations nor does the sequence reflect any technological order. The original DF-1 was significantly more advanced than the DF-2, while the DF-3 was a 10,000km-range ICBM.

The unrealistic plans of the Great Leap Forward eventually yielded to reality and so did early plans for the development of a Chinese ICBM. Work on the earliest missiles proceeded slowly, culminating in the failure of the first DF-2 flight test in March 1962. Chinese histories of the period note that the failures allowed Nie to reorientate the development of the missile programme along more rational lines.[4]

China successfully tested the medium-range DF-2 in a series of launches in June–July 1964, followed by the 1966 test of a DF-2 with a live nuclear warhead. The successful tests occurred against the backdrop of a gradual reform of China's plans to develop ballistic missiles. These reforms occurred in piecemeal fashion, although in retrospect they appear to represent a turning point in the programme to develop ballistic missiles. China ultimately abandoned the old DF-3 ICBM. In its place, the old DF-1 was reimagined as a follow-on to the DF-2, taking over the DF-3 designation. (China retroactively designated the now obsolete 1059 missile as the DF-1.) This turn culminated in a March 1965 reorganisation of China's plans to develop an ICBM by 1975. Under this plan, China sought to develop four missiles in eight years (*Banian Sidan*).[5]

This plan proposed two new missiles to be designated the DF-4 and the DF-5.[6]

Some accounts describe China's first generation of ballistic missiles – the DF-2, DF-3, DF-4 and DF-5 – in terms of range aspirations: the ability to strike Japan, followed by the Philippines, then Guam, and ultimately the continental US. While Chinese designers were given notional targets, the real innovation embodied in the *Banian Sidan* plan was the structuring of the ICBM programme around incremental technical goals. In retrospect, the DF-1 represented successful copy production, while the DF-2 was an indigenised Soviet missile. The subsequent missiles represented technical accomplishments as much as anything else. The DF-3 represented the first effort to cluster engines and use storable propellant (unsymmetrical dimethylhydrazine instead of liquid oxygen). The DF-4 represented the first effort at staging, using a DF-3 as a first stage. Ultimately, the DF-5 integrated all these technical achievements into a full-range ICBM, making a number of technical improvements that allowed Chinese designers to create the massive missile.[7]

China completed these developmental goals in order, and largely on time, except in the case of the DF-5, where the successful test in 1971 was followed by a long period of disruption amid the Cultural Revolution. China conducted a full-range DF-5 test in 1980 as part of the 'three grasps' campaign to complete the unfinished business of the 1960s and 1970s – an operational ICBM, a submarine-launched ballistic missile (SLBM), and a communications satellite.[8]

It should be noted that the completion of initial flight-testing for a given missile did not signal the end of its development. Flight testing appears to have continued as long as a missile was in service, though after deployment flight tests moved from research organisations, such as the China Academy of Launch Technology, to the operational tests by either the Second Artil-

Table 4. **China's First Generation of Liquid-fuelled Ballistic Missiles**

Name	Old	US	Initial testing cycles
DF-1	1059	none	November–December 1960
DF-2	DF-2	CSS-1	June–July 1964
DF-3	DF-1	CSS-2	December 1966–May 1967 (December 1985–1986)
DF-4	none	CSS-3	November 1969–January 1970 (May 1975)
DF-5	none	CSS-4	September 1971, May 1980

lery's equipment department or operational brigades.[9] China continued to make evolutionary improvements following the successful production of a missile. So, for example, after DF-3 testing and deployment, China conducted a second flight-test series in the mid-1980s to produce the DF-3A.

Establishing the Second Artillery Corps

China did not match the quick development of the DF series of ballistic missiles with deployments of operational missile units. It tested the DF-3, -4 and -5 in the late 1960s and early 1970s, but debates about basing modes lasted through the 1970s, with deployments stretching into the 1980s. China did not begin to equip subordinate units with its first true ICBM, the DF-5, until the late 1980s. Deployment of this system was completed in May 1995.

China established the Second Artillery in 1966, using units from the artillery that had been equipped with Soviet-supplied short-range missiles and from a department of the Ministry of Public Security (a forerunner of the paramilitary People's Armed Police). It established the first launch regiments by 1968. During this period, China recalled engineering units from Southeast Asia, which had been aiding north Vietnam, to assist in the construction of underground and hardened facilities.[10]

The early years of the Second Artillery were marked by factional infighting that reflected the disparate artillery and security elements, as well as the broader factionalism that characterised the Cultural Revolution. Lewis and Xue recount the turbulent early history of the Second Artillery through the travails of its first commander, Xiang Shouzhi, who came from the artillery.[11] As outlined in Chapter One, Xiang ran afoul of Lin Biao, who used the October 1969 evacuation of Beijing to place Xiang under house arrest at a farm. Xiang was recalled to lead the Second Artillery in the mid-1970s, only to be sent away again.[12] When asked to return a third time, Xiang opted to stay in Nanjing. He reportedly added that tending to pigs was more appealing than returning for another stint at the helm of the Second Artillery.

Despite claims that China may have deployed some ballistic missiles during the mid-1960s, the US did not detect troop training of ballistic-missile units until 1969. (Second Artillery units conduct such training at missile test centres, rather than at deployment sites, presumably to preserve operational secrecy regarding the locations of deployed units.)[13] As late as the early 1970s, the US had not identified any deployed missile units. As a result, it remains unclear when China first deployed missiles and nuclear weapons for use with the Second Artillery, nor is it clear if China had any operational missile units during the 1969 crisis with the Soviet Union or plans for retaliation involving assets at missile test facilities and training centres.

China spent much of the 1970s establishing basing modes for the first generation of ballistic missiles. It is not possible to store ballistic missiles with their volatile and corrosive propellants for any length of time.[14] As a consequence, the process of arming, erecting, aiming, fuelling and firing these missiles can take hours, during which the missiles are extremely vulnerable to attack.

The pre-launch exposure of the DF-3, for example, is said to be between three and four hours. China based its DF-3 ballistic missiles in caves or hardened shelters, from which they could be transported to presurveyed launch sites.

The two-stage DF-4 and DF-5 presented more challenges regarding basing. These missiles are so large that they lack even the severely limited mobility of the DF-3. Chinese designers initially planned to base the DF-4 in a silo-like structure containing an elevator that would lift the missile above ground where it could be launched. China's weaponeers became acutely aware of the growing vulnerability of silos to more accurate enemy missiles. During the mid-1970s, China changed the basing mode of the DF-4, deciding to place the missiles, propellant and other equipment in caves from which the missile would 'roll out' to launch. China also examined a number of alternative basing modes for the DF-4, including trials for rail-basing. The first operational DF-4 rollout-to-launch site, near Da Qaidam in Qinghai, became operational in 1982. China ultimately constructed ten to twelve rollout-to-launch sites for the DF-4, as well as two elevate-to-launch silos.

The Chinese considered similar basing modes for the DF-5, but ultimately concluded rail-basing and other modes were impractical. China deployed a pair of DF-5 ballistic missiles in silos in 1981. It did not make significant deployments until the late 1980s and early 1990s, when the number of silo-based DF-5s grew from around six to 18.

China's basing modes relied heavily on camouflage for protection. Often Chinese engineering units erected camouflaged netting to hide construction of cave entrances and silos. In many cases, these nets were strung across narrow mountain valleys.

From an examination of declassified US intelligence documents, the US seems to have detected most of these sites during periods of construction. Camouflage netting often had the opposite effect, drawing the interest of the photo analysts. Other signatures were simply too difficult to hide – encampments to house workers, barracks for troops and rail shipment of equipment, materials, and ultimately the missiles themselves. One example relates to a site near Lushi.[15] The US detected construction of a silo at this location in mid-1982, initially believing it was for the DF-4.[16] After observing rail traffic – China transported missile airframes in specialised rail-cars – and the silo during a period when camouflage had been removed, the US concluded by the end of 1984 that the silo was for the DF-5.[17]

Looking at these sites today, the locations are well camou-flaged. Simple camouflage may be detectable using intel-ligence satellites with synthetic aperture radar (SAR) and near-field infrared sensors, but the PLA has responded with its own investments, establishing a Second Artillery research institute dedicated to camouflage, concealment and decep-tion. Declassified US intelligence reports suggest that the period of construction is the point at which a site is most likely to be compromised.

Developing solid-fuelled missiles

During the 1980s, China shifted its emphasis toward the devel-opment of solid-fuelled missiles. Research had begun on a two-stage solid-fuelled missile in 1967. The programme seemed driven largely by a desire to have what others have – in this case an SLBM – with little consideration of the strategic or operational implications of such a weapon. Work proceeded slowly during the 1970s, culminating in a March 1985 meeting where Nie's deputy and successor, Zhang Aiping, apparently ridiculed the notion of a sea-based deterrent by arguing that a Chinese submarine armed with the JL-1 would have to travel to the Arabian Sea for Moscow to be within range.[18] China subse-quently emphasised the land-based variant, the DF-21.

China continued with the SLBM programme, listing it as one of the 'three grasps' needed to conclude the unfinished business of China's first generation of strategic programme. The first JL-1 test occurred in October 1982. China's *Xia*-class SSBN went to sea in 1983.[19]

In the mid-1980s, Deng Xiaoping extended the timeline for the construction of the second submarine, a decision that amounted to its cancellation. The *Xia*-class submarine has never gone on patrol. It is usually described as not operational and not deployed, although in a crisis situation Chinese leaders might have ordered the submarine armed with nuclear weapons and sent out to sea.

Completion of the 'three grasps' fulfilled China's first generation of strategic goals. The second generation focused on the development of land-based missiles in the form of solid-fuelled mobile ballistic missiles. In January 1985 the State Council and Central Military Commission outlined a second generation of strategic weapons: DF-21/JL-1 to replace the DF-3; DF-31/JL-2 to replace the DF-4; and the DF-41 to replace the DF-5. China developed a land-based variant of the JL-1, successfully testing the DF-21 in 1985.[20] However, the widespread conversion of DF-3 units to DF-21 units did not begin until the late 1990s.

After China tested the DF-21 in May 1985, it began a range extension programme in August 1985 that ultimately produced the DF-21A. (Development on the JL-1 appears to have stopped after an aborted programme in the mid-1980s to develop underwater ignition.[21]) Testing on the DF-21 continued through the mid-1990s, with deployments beginning in the mid-1990s at Tonghua and subsequently Chuxiong, continuing through the mid-2000s.[22]

While research and development of the DF-31/JL-2 began in the mid-1980s, flight testing of the DF-31 did not begin until August 1999.[23] DF-31 flight testing was probably completed by the mid-2000s. Development of the sea-based variant, the JL-2, was more difficult. China suffered a series of testing failures relating to the JL-2, until the most recent cycle of testing in August 2012, which appears to have been successful.[24]

Initially, the DF-41 programme appears to have given way to a range-extended DF-31, called the DF-31A. Testing on the DF-31A continued through to at least June 2007.[25]

The US intelligence community now believes China is developing a new road-mobile ICBM that may be capable of carrying multiple warheads.[26] According to press reports, China first tested this missile in 2013.[27] It is unclear whether the Chinese will designate the new missile the DF-41 or, if they do, whether the designation is simply recycled. Claims that the missile may carry as many as ten warheads are difficult to credit, given the reported size of China's most modern nuclear weapon and the throw-weight of even modern Russian solid-fuelled ICBMs.

While China largely replaced the older liquid-fueled DF-3 with the more modern, solid-fueled DF-21, it elected to retain the liquid fueled DF-4 and DF-5 ICBMs, even as solid-fueled replacements in the form of the DF-31 and DF-31A have become available. China conducted a programme to enhance the DF-5, deploying a new modification during the mid-2000s.[28] The US intelligence community calls this missile the CSS-4 Mod 2. The replacement of the DF-5 with the DF-5A in the mid-2000s may have reflected the slow development of the DF-31A, which continued in flight testing through at least June 2007. As noted in Chapter Two, China's DF-5 ballistic missile is the main candidate for carrying multiple warheads, particularly if China chooses to deploy its most modern warhead, developed for the DF-31, on older liquid-fuelled missiles such as the DF-5.

China is also taking steps to improve the ability of its nuclear forces to penetrate missile defences. In January 2014, and again in August, China tested a hypersonic glide vehicle – although the August test appears to have been a failure.[29] The US National Air and Space Intelligence Center has stated

China's nuclear navy

Although Chinese documents, such as the Defense White Paper, refer to the Second Artillery as China's 'main' nuclear force, China developed a ballistic-missile submarine (the *Xia*) and submarine-launched ballistic missile, *Julang* (Great Wave) -1, in the mid-1980s. China's ballistic-missile submarines, as well as China's new aircraft carrier, may reflect the long-running influence of the late admiral Liu Huaqing, a former PLAN chief and eventually a vice chairman of the Central Military Commission (CMC).[31]

US intelligence assessments usually list the JL-1 as not deployed, but the precise status of the lone Type 092 *Xia*-class submarine is unclear. According to Eugene Habiger, former commander of US Strategic Command, the *Xia* 'went on one cruise and has been essentially in dry dock ever since.' However, the submarine was overhauled in 1995–1998 and a recent Xinhua retrospective contained a number of images of the *Xia* participating in exercises at sea.[32] It is possible that the best description of the submarine is a prolonged form of 'trial operational deployment' similar to the early deployments of the DF-4 and DF-5. The *Xia*-class submarine may not be operational, but it is presumably available in extremis for limited missions.

China's new class of ballistic-missile submarines, the Type 094 *Jin*-class, appears to represent a more serious effort to take China's deterrent to sea. China has constructed four *Jin*-class boats. The *Jin*-class is reportedly much quieter than the *Xia*. Charts released by the Office of Naval Intelligence suggest that it is comparable in radiated noise to the Soviet *Delta* I submarines that went to sea in the early 1970s.[33] This estimate is consistent with the stated displacement of the *Jin*-class submarine, which is larger than the *Xia*. Submarines have to be made larger in order to accommodate sound-isolating mounts.

China's new SSBNs are based at the Yulin Naval Base on Hainan. To bring the continental US within range of the 7,000–8,000km-range JL-2, the *Jin* must go to sea, transiting through straits and passages to the open ocean of the north Pacific.

Technical considerations, such as the range of the JL-2 and China's apparently limited infrastructure for communicating with its ballistic missile submarines, raise a number of questions about possible operational patterns for the *Jin*-class SSBNs once they are armed with JL-2 missiles.[34] It is unclear whether China will maintain a continuous at-sea deterrent through constant patrolling – as the US, UK and France do – or whether China will conduct patrols on a more episodic basis, as Russia does. If China's naval posture mirrors the land-based force, one might expect that China's submarines would be put to sea with nuclear weapons infrequently, with China perhaps flushing them to sea in a crisis.

that the hypersonic glide vehicle under development 'is associated with [China's] nuclear deterrent forces'.[30] A hypersonic vehicle would help Chinese nuclear warheads evade American missile defences.

China is also developing a sea-based variant of the DF-31 called the JL-2. China has constructed at least four *Jin*-class ballistic missile submarines, each of which can carry 12 JL-2 SLBMs. Delays in the JL-2 programme, however, have slowed deployment of this system (see box on 'China's nuclear navy' on the previous page).

Growing importance of conventionally armed ballistic missiles

While China has enhanced the survivability of its nuclear deterrent with the deployment of mobile, solid-fuelled ballistic missiles, the most important cultural change within the Second Artillery has been the development and deployment of conventionally armed missiles. Westerners tend to think of the Second Artillery as China's nuclear force, but today conventionally armed missiles account for the majority of its inventory of missiles and launchers, as well as about half the brigades. Nuclear missions play a declining role in the broader portfolio of Second Artillery capabilities, a shift that has far-reaching implications.

A disproportionate number of these brigades – at least six – remain orientated toward a Taiwan scenario, with Chinese textbooks and other materials suggesting a more offensive role for conventional missile forces than nuclear forces shackled to a no-first-use policy.

The earliest indications of China's interest in conventionally armed ballistic missiles appeared in the context of the Iran–Iraq War during the 1980s. China developed conventionally armed variants of the DF-3, as well as new short-range ballistic missiles (SRBM) for export. In 1987, China sold convention-ally armed DF-3 missiles, training and other services to Saudi Arabia, followed by a series of missile sales to Pakistan.[35] Recent reports suggest China sold DF-21, and possibly other ballistic missiles, to Saudi Arabia around 2007.[36]

China subsequently deployed for itself the short-range missiles sold to Pakistan, naming them the DF-11 (CSS-7) and DF-15 (CSS-6). These two missiles represent the bulk of China's inventory of conventionally armed SRBMs. In the late 1990s, China had 'fewer than fifty' such launchers. By 2009, the number had grown to more than 200.[37] Since convention-ally armed missile units have multiple missiles per launcher, the total inventory is probably about 1,000 DF-11 and DF-15 missiles.[38] Not all of these missiles are necessarily deployed for use with military units.

China is developing a large number of new SRBMs, includ-ing the 800km-range DF-16 (CSS-11). Many of the new missile types fall well below the Missile Technology Control Regime (MTCR) threshold of a maximum 500kg payload and a 300km range. These systems are largely intended for export (they lack, for example, DF- designations.). If deployed, these systems will serve as long-range artillery, comparable to the US Army Tactical Missile System (ATACMS). These systems include the CSS-8, -9, -14, -15 and -16.

China developed conventional and anti-ship variants of the DF-21 (DF-21C and DF-21D respectively), and the DH-10 (sometimes CJ-10) cruise missile. An air-launched variant could arm new variants of China's H-6 bomber.

The death in 2005 of Yang Yegong, the commander of the Second Artillery's Base 52, offers an interesting insight into the cultural evolution of the Second Artillery. Yang Yegong received an unusual amount of attention in Chinese state media for his contributions to the development of China's national defence, which appears to have been largely in the area of conventional missile capabilities.[39]

Doctrinal texts, such as the *Science of Campaigns* and the *Science of Second Artillery Campaigns*, describe conventional missile operations in very different terms from nuclear ones. Conventional missile operations emphasise striking first to gain initiative, a doctrine at odds with no-first-use policy that sometimes leads to confusion.

As China deploys large numbers of conventional missiles and articulates a doctrine for the use of conventional missile power that emphasised their early use, some analysts have interpreted the changes in China's conventional missile forces as a harbinger of changes to China's nuclear policies, including the possibility of a sprint to numerical parity and abandonment of no-first-use.

An alternative possibility is that the growing emphasis on conventional missile operations reflects a declining role for nuclear weapons in the Second Artillery. With the passage of time, large deployments of conventional missiles have not been matched with comparable deployments of nuclear-armed systems. Nor has China created the new launch brigades and, most likely, bases, that would be necessary to accommodate a significant expansion in nuclear-armed missiles. Increasingly, the Second Artillery appears organised to conduct conventional missile campaigns.

China's current nuclear-missile force

Of China's large number of ballistic and cruise missiles, only a portion are deployed with nuclear weapons. In this context, 'deployed with' means that the missile unit has available nuclear weapons maintained by a specialised regimental-level unit at a 'nearby' location. In the case of the DF-5, the term 'nearby' appears to mean tens of kilometres.

Second Artillery force structure

The force structure of the Second Artillery is more complicated than a simple table showing the number of missile launchers or missiles. Far more than a single truck is needed to conduct a launch operation. A brigade of missile launchers requires support vehicles, as well as an infrastructure to maintain the vehicles, missiles and warheads, to say nothing of the infrastructure necessary to support the people who perform these tasks. As a result, it is necessary to consider the Second Artillery as an organisation.

China's new transporter-erector launchers

Since 2009, China has steadily replaced the old-style transporter-erector launcher (TEL) with its DF-15 and DF-21 ballistic missiles, with new-style TELs produced by the Wanshan Special Vehicle Company (WSV). WSV-produced TELs are clearly different in style from previous Chinese TELs and resemble those manufactured by MAZ/MZKT in Belarus, Wanshan's joint-venture partner. (This firm is responsible for the export of heavy-duty chassis to North Korea, which were modified to carry the KN-08 intercontinental-range ballistic missile.) China has paraded the DF-31 and DF-31A in old-style TELs, leading to speculation that new vehicles will appear for China's road-mobile, nuclear-armed ICBMs.

In 2013–14, Chinese bloggers posted images of at least three new-style TELs and their respective missile canisters that do not correspond to known missiles. These images depict a TEL with at least six axles, a six-axle TEL, and an eight-axle TEL.

The photographs appear to show three TELs that are clearly larger than known TELs for the DF-11, DF-15 or DF-21. The angles on the photographs are poor and in some cases key features are obscured, either deliberately or through hasty photography. These TELs appear to be for three different missiles, such as a new TEL for the DF-31/DF-31A or for the expected DF-41.

The Second Artillery is commanded by a full general, who has been a member of the Central Military Commission since 2004. The Second Artillery political commissar holds a grade equal to a military region commander, but chairs the Second

Artillery Party Committee. The commander serves as vice chair-man of the Party Committee.[40] The Second Artillery is divided into six bases (sometimes armies), numbered 51–56, each led by an officer equal in grade to a corps leader.[41] Bases 51–56 oversee subordinate launch brigades and support regiments. The Second Artillery command oversees a separate base, Base 22, which is responsible for maintaining the stockpile of nuclear warheads. The leadership also oversees at least three training bases, and an engineering base headquartered at Luoyang in Henan province. The engineering base, which was established in 2012, oversees a command in Hanzhong, Shaanxi, that is primarily responsible for tunnelling, a co-located 'engineering technology general group' in Luoyang, responsible for facility installation, and a specialised engineering brigade for disaster response that is garrisoned north of Beijing.[42]

Each base responsible for ballistic- or cruise-missile deploy-ments has between three and six subordinate brigades. The exception is Base 52, which operates conventional missiles, and may have nine missile brigades. This structure represents stan-dard military thinking about hierarchy and span of control. It exerts command from the base, down through brigades, battal-ions, companies and platoons.[43]

Each brigade, for example, operates a limited number of launchers maintained by launch battalions and/or launch compa-nies. A launch platform in this context can be a silo (as in the case of the DF-5), a rollout-to-launch site (such as for the DF-4) or, for mobile missiles, a transporter-erector launcher (TEL). The missiles and launchers require significant support embodied in the personnel of the company, battalion and brigade.

The structure of brigades differs for fixed-site missiles and mobile missiles, as well as for conventional and nuclear missiles. As a result, the number of missiles per brigade may vary greatly between conventional missiles (up to 36 launchers with as many as six missiles per launcher), mobile nuclear-armed missiles (between six and 12 missile launchers per brigade), and fixed-site nuclear-armed missiles (six or fewer silos or cave rollout sites). This reflects differences in the number of battalions, companies and launchers assigned to each unit.

When looking at unclassified US estimates, it usually makes sense to estimate that each nuclear-armed mobile missile brigade has approximately eight launchers, although this very rough approximation does not necessarily reflect each unit or missile type. So, for example, the National Air and Space Intelligence Center (NASIC) assesses that China has '5–10' DF-31 missiles and 'more than 15' DF-31A missiles.[44] Using an average of eight, China probably has one DF-31 brigade and two DF-31A brigades.

With the structure of bases, brigades and launch units, a rough order of battle for the Second Artillery is set out in Table 5.

Each base and brigade has a headquarters, with multiple subordinate launch units. As suggested by the use of cave-based rollout sites, the Second Artillery relies extensively on underground facilities and engineering elements responsible for digging them. Launch units are based above ground on a day-to-day basis in peacetime. Underground facilities are used for storage, as well as missile-warhead assembly, check-out, and rollout. Chinese launch units practise deploying to tunnels for short periods of time, as they would if riding out a nuclear attack in line with the country's no-first-use policy. A Xinhua article described a 'multiday survival training' exercise in which a launch battalion spent eight days living in a tunnel, before conducting a launch exercise.[45] The focus of the article concerns the 'poor living environment' of the tunnels for even short periods of time, particularly the challenge of maintaining nutrition. For example, cooked meals are prohibited because the heat from a kitchen would reveal the tunnel is occupied.[46]

Table 5. **Notional Order of Battle for the Second Artillery**

Base	Brigade	MUCD	PLACE	MISSILE
51	HQ	96101	Shenyang, Liaoning	
	806	96111	Hancheng, Shaanxi	DF-21A
	810	96113	Dalian, Liaoning	DF-3/21A
	816	96115	Tonghua, Jilin	DF-21
	822	96117	Laiwu, Shandong	DF-21C
	UI	96119	Qingzhou, Shandong	DF-21C?
52	HQ	96151	Huangshan, Anhui	
	807	96161	Chizhou, Anhui	DF-21A
	811	96163	Jingdezhen, Jiangxi	DF-21C
	815	96165	Leping, Jingdezhen, Jiangxi or Shangrao, Jiangxi	DF-15
	817	96167	Yong'an, Sanming, Fujian	DF-11A
	818	96169	Meizhou, Guangdong	DF-11A
	819	96162	Ganzhou, Jianxi	DF-15
	820	96164	Jinhua, Zhejiang	DF-15
	826	96166	Shaoguan, Guangdong	DF-16?
	UI	91618	Xianyou, Putian, Fujian	DF-11
53	HQ	96201	Kunming, Yunnan	
	802	96211	Jianshu, Yunnan	DF-21A
	808	96213	Chuxiong, Yuannan or Yuxi, Yunnan	DF-21C/DF-31
	821	96215	Liuzhou, Guangxi	DH-10
	UI	96212	Puning, Jieyang, Guangdong	DF-11
	825	96219	Qingyuan, Guangdong	DF-21D?
	UI	96217	Qingzhen, Guizhou	Training Bde
54	HQ	96251	Luoyang, Henan	
	801	96261	Lingbao, Sanmenxia, Henan	DF-5A
	804	96263	Luoning, Henan	DF-5A
	813	96265	Nanyang, Henan	DF-31
		96267	Xinyang	
55	HQ	96301	Huaihua, Hunan	
	803	96311	Jingzhou, Huaihua, Hunan	DF-5A
	805	96313	Shaoyang, Hunan	DF-31A
	814	96315	Huitong, Hunan	DF-5A
	824	96317	Yichun, Jiangxi	DH-10
56	HQ	96351	Xining, Qinghai	
	809	96361	Datong County, Qinghai	DF-21
	812	96363	Tianshui, Gansu	DF-31A
	UI (823)	96365	Kuerla, Xinjiang	DF-21C
		96367	Delinghua, Qinghai	Training Bde

In some instances, two local names are given if the base is located within a prefecture-level city like Sanmenxia or Huaihua. Author estimates based on Directory of PRC Military Personalities (various editions). See also Mark A. Stokes, Second Artillery Unit and Leadership Directory 2014, 2 January 2014. Many thanks to Henry Boyd for valuable comments on the order of battle.

As a result of such hardships, units do not appear to spend significant time underground. Each Second Artillery element lives in above-ground barracks and facilities, deploying to temporary shelters only for short exercises and in the event of an emergency.

These organisational factors allow monitoring of China's overall deployment of ballistic missiles. So, for example, the US intelligence community monitored the process of replacing the DF-3 with the DF-21 by watching as units stopped training, then received new barracks and other above-ground facilities to support the more mobile DF-21. One consequence of the shift from the DF-3 to the DF-21, as well as the addition of the DF-31 and DF-31A, has been a reconfiguration of many Chinese bases, many of which are now in new locations.

In addition to the forces of the Second Artillery, the Chinese Navy (PLAN) has built four *Jin*-class ballistic-missile submarines in the past decade, based in Hainan.[47] Each *Jin*-class submarine has 12 launch tubes to carry the JL-2 SLBM. Despite the appearance of the *Jin*-class submarines, the slow development of the JL-2 ballistic missile has delayed deployment of the sea-based deterrent.[48] Major operational questions, such as how China would communicate with ballistic submarines and whether China would conduct continuous patrols, remain unanswered. It is not clear, for example, whether Chinese naval units will control nuclear warheads outside of the Second Artillery Base 22 structure during peacetime, or whether units assigned to PLAN fleets would receive warheads only in a crisis.

China probably does not maintain aircraft-delivered or tactical nuclear weapons. During the 1970s and 1980s, the US was unable to identify locations at airfields for nuclear-weapons storage, nor were there accounts of warhead handling for units other than ballistic missiles.[49] Some estimates periodically list aircraft as having secondary nuclear missions, or speculate that China may have an interest in tactical nuclear weapons, but the evidence for such deployments is very scant.

Operational practices

The major operational shift in nuclear operations for the Second Artillery has been moving from hardened sites with liquid-fuelled ballistic missiles to mobile operations using solid-fuelled ballistic missiles.

China's liquid-fuelled ballistic missiles are not kept fuelled during peacetime. A typical rollout-to-launch exercise for a DF-4, presented on China Central Television (CCTV), demonstrates the operational aspects of launching Chinese liquid-fuelled ballistic missiles.[50] The launch exercise is located at a training centre, as suggested by the fact that the building in which the warhead is attached is above ground. Chinese missileers must arm the warhead inside its shelter and complete a checkout of the missile. The missile is then rolled out to the launchpad, where it is erected. The missile is fuelled and guidance sets are aligned and programmed. Preparations can take hours to complete.

The DF-3 (CSS-2) had limited mobility. The introduction of the truly mobile DF-21, DF-31 and DF-31A, on the other hand, has resulted in new operational practices for the Second Artillery. Mobile operations can be seen in satellite images near Da Qaidam, which previously contained two cave rollout-to-launch sites, and now may be a training centre.

During peacetime, a unit is located in a garrison. In the event of a crisis, the garrison is a likely target of enemy attack. On strategic warning, the unit could deploy to a hardened shelter, a holding area, or proceed directly to a launch site. There are a number of launch sites along the main road stretching from a garrison location. In satellite images of Da Qaidam, one can clearly see the pad during periods when it is unoccupied, as well as when it contains vehicles covered in netting and tents or conducting a launch exercise.

China appears to continue to store nuclear warheads separately from ballistic missiles during peacetime. A description of a mobile missile launched in the Gobi desert – likely at the Da Qaidam training area – describes the unit mating the RV to the missile on the fifth day of the exercise, following manoeuvres in the field, then erecting and launching the missile, though it would seem more typical for units to mate warheads before deployment.[51]

The Second Artillery has an extensive system for handling warheads, centred on Base 22 near Baoji in Shaanxi province.[52] Each launch base has units that replicate these functions, with a warhead regiment. China initially stored nuclear weapons in three vaults west of the original nuclear-weapons design facility near Haiyan (Koko Nor). Sometime after the late 1960s, warhead storage moved to the Second Artillery unit near Baoji. Base 22 is responsible for storing warheads, transporting them, training units in warhead handling, communications, and maintenance of warheads and special vehicles. The size and composition of these units has remained roughly the same, suggesting that new Second Artillery brigades are largely armed with conventional warheads.

Conclusion

China's development of an operational ballistic-missile force occurred much more slowly, and in a more vulnerable way, than is normally imagined. A recurring theme of US and Chinese dialogues on strategic stability has been Western scepticism that China truly has a survivable force. It is not difficult to understand this scepticism, given the small number of missiles, as well as their basing modes.

In particular, China has relied heavily on tunneling and camouflage to protect relatively small nuclear forces. The US approach, by contrast, has emphasised large deployments that ensure survivability through sheer numbers. Little effort is made to hide US missile silos. When the US considered more survivable basing modes for what would become the *Peace-keeper* missile, it considered multiple protective shelters (the so-called 'shell game'), but again did not plan to make efforts to hide deployment areas.

The vulnerability of the Second Artillery is exacerbated by the policy of riding out a first strike, as well as the long times associated with moving units into launch areas and arming missiles with nuclear warheads. China's apparent solution to this problem is to put their forces on alert in a crisis situation,

Table 6. **China Ballistic Missiles**

US Designation	Chinese	Propellant	Mode	Range (km)	No. of Launchers
CSS-2 Mod 2	DF-3A	Liquid	Transportable	3,000	5–10 (limited mobility)
CSS-3	DF-4	Liquid	Silo & transportable	5,500+	10–15
CSS-4 Mod 2	DF-5A	Liquid	Silo	12,000+	About 20
CSS-5 Mod 1	DF-21	Solid	Road-mobile	1,750+	Fewer than 50
CSS-5 Mod 2	DF-21A	Solid	Road-mobile	1,750+	
CSS-5 Conventional	DF-21C	Solid	Road-mobile	1,750+	Fewer than 30
CSS-5 Mod 5	DF-21D			1,500+	Unknown
CSS-6 Mod 1	DF-15/M-9	Solid	Road-mobile	600	
CSS-6 Mod 2	DF-15A	Solid	Road-mobile	850+	90–110
CSS-6 Mod 3	DF-15B	Solid	Road-mobile	750+	
CSS-7 Mod 1	DF-11/M-11	Solid	Road-mobile	300	120–140
CSS-7 Mod 2	DF-11A	Solid	Road-mobile	600	
CSS-8	B610	Solid/liquid	Road-mobile	150	
CSS-9 Mod 1	B611	Solid	Road-mobile	150	Dual launcher
CSS-9 Mod-X-2	B611M	Solid	Road-mobile	260	
CSS-10 Mod 1	DF-31	Solid	Road-mobile	7,000+	5-10
CSS-10 Mod 2	DF-31A	Solid	Road-mobile	11,000+	More than 15
CSS-11 Mod 1	DF-16	Solid	Road-mobile	800+	
CSS-14 Mod-X-1	P12	Solid	Road-mobile	150	Dual-launcher
CSS-14 Mod-X-2	BP12A	Solid	Road-mobile	280	
CSS-X-15	M20	Solid	Road-mobile	280	
CSS-X-16	SY400	Solid	Road-mobile	200	8 rocket MLRS
CSS-NX-3	JL-1	Solid	Submarine-launched	1,700+	Not yet deployed
CSS-NX-14	JL-2	Solid	Submarine-launched	7,000+	Not yet deployed
	YJ-63		LACM		
	DH-10		LACM		

both to reduce their vulnerability and to signal China's resolve to an adversary. As the next chapter will explore, this approach runs some risk of escalating a crisis, particularly if Washington or Moscow misinterprets alert operations as the early stages of an attack.

Notes

1   Lewis and Xue, *China Builds the Bomb* (Stanford University Press, 1988), pp. 70–71.

2   'Annual Report to Congress: Military and Security Developments Involving the People's Republic of China 2012', US Department of Defense, May 2012, p. 24, http://www.defense.gov/pubs/pdfs/2012_cmpr_final.pdf.

3   'China Nuclear Force Commander Reiterates "No First Use" Policy To Codel Skelton', http://www.cablegatesearch.net/cable.php?id=07BEIJING5707&version=1314919461.

4   *China Today: Defense Science and Industry* (Beijing, National Defense University Press, 1993) p. 65.

5   The fact that the DF-1 was an SS-2 copy accounts for a discrepancy in Chinese and US designations – the DF-2 is the CSS-1, the DF-3 is the CSS-2, and so on. US designations are based on the order in which a missile system was identified. Having the designations so close can often result in confusion.

6   Thus, the DF-3 of the post-1964 era bears no relationship to the missile that bore the designation.

7   The Chinese distinguish ranges slightly differently than Americans. Whereas the US defines the DF-4 and DF-5 as ICBMs, China distinguishes between the two.

8   Evan Feigenbaum, *China's Technowarriors: National Security and Strategic Competition from the Nuclear to the Information Age* (Stanford, CA: Stanford University Press, 2003), p. 79.

9   I am indebted to Mark Stokes for this observation.

10 *Ibid.*

11 Lewis and Litai, *Imagined Enemies*, p. 175.

12 According to Lewis and Xue, Xiang was an opponent of the radicals, but moderates interpreted his efforts to mend fences with Jiang Qing as a secret effort to ingratiate himself with the Gang of Four.

13 China makes little effort to hide troop training at such locations. One of the current DF-31 training sites, for example, is near Kangzhuang. On a hillside overlooking the site are massive characters that read 'Build an eco-friendly test range'. China has also released videos showing units training at such locations.

14 Accidents involving the *Titan* II at Searcy, Arkansas in 1965, Rock, Kansas in 1978, and Damascus, Arkansas in 1980 demonstrate the challenges of maintaining fuelled missiles in launch-ready status. For a readable account of the 1980 accident

at Damascus, see Eric Schlosser, *Command and Control: Nuclear Weapons, the Damascus Accident, and the Illusion of Safety* (New York: The Penguin Press, 2013).

15   Recently declassified US intelligence documents provide details.

16   'Identification of Probable CSS-3 Rollout, Erect-to-Launch Site, Lushi Probably SSM Launch Site 3, China', CIA, 14 October 1982, approved for release 12 January 2011.

17   'CSS-4 Upper Silo Configuration, Lushi SSM Launch Site 3, China', CIA, December 1984, approved for release 20 July 2010.

18   Lewis and Hua, *China's Strategic Seapower*, p. 27.

19   *Ibid.*, p. 120.

20   *Ibid.*, p. 188.

21   *Ibid.*

22   This date is much later than is usually given. Flight testing and conversion of barracks are detailed in classified documents leaked to Bill Gertz of the *Washington Times*. China conducted two DF-21 flight tests in 1995 and 1996. The first deployments were described in a November 1996 document that expected conversion to be complete by 2002. The Office of the Secretary of Defense indicated that the DF-21 had largely replaced the DF-3, which remained deployed by a single brigade by 2005. See 'Annual Report to Congress: The Military Power of the People's Republic of China 2005', Office of the Secretary of Defense, http://www.defense.gov/news/Jul2005/d20050719china.pdf.

23   Kenneth H. Bacon, 'DoD News Briefing', US Department of Defense, 12 December 2000, http://www.defense.gov/transcripts/transcript.aspx?transcriptid=1876.

24   On failure, see 'Annual Report to Congress: Military and Security Developments Involving the People's Republic of China 2010', Office of the Secretary of Defense, p. 34, http://www.defense.gov/pubs/pdfs/2010_cmpr_final.pdf; on technical hurdles, see 'Annual Report to Congress: Military and Security Developments Involving the People's Republic of China 2011', Office of the Secretary of Defense, pp. 34, 62, http://www.defense.gov/pubs/pdfs/2011_cmpr_final.pdf; on success in 2012, see 'Annual Report to Congress: Military and Security Developments Involving the People's Republic of China 2013', Office of the Secretary of Defense, p. 31, http://www.defense.gov/pubs/2013_china_report_final.pdf.

25   'Delhi Diary, July 17–25', http://www.cablegatesearch.net/cable.php?id=07NEWDELHI3383.

26   'Annual Report to Congress: Military and Security Developments Involving the People's Republic of China 2013'.

27   Bill Gertz, 'China Conducts Second Flight Test of New Long-Range Missile', *Washington Free Beacon*, 17 December 2013.

28   Lewis and Hua, 'China's Ballistic Missile Programs', p. 29.

29   For a technical analysis of the apparently failed August test, see James Acton, Catherine Dill and Jeffrey Lewis, *Crashing Glider, Hidden Hotspring: Analyzing China's August 7, 2014 Hypersonic Glider Test*, Arms Control Wonk, 3 September 2014, http://lewis.armscontrolwonk.com/archive/7443/crashing-glider-hidden-hotspring.

30 Donald L. Fuell, technical director for force modernisation and employment, National Air and Space Intelligence Center, quoted in 'China's Military Modernization and its Implications for the United States', hearing before the US–China Economic And Security Review Commission, 30 January 2014, p. 36

31 Liu also helped to preserve funding for the human space-flight programme. See Jeffrey Lewis and Gregory Kulacki, 'A Place for One's Mat: China's Space Program: 1956–2003', American Academy of Arts & Sciences, 2009, p. 25.

32 'Inside PLA Navy's 1t nuclear-powered sub force', China Daily, 27 October 2013, http://www.chinadaily.com.cn/slides/2013-10/27/content_17061925_2.htm.

33 The charts, released in 1996 and 2007, redact the noise levels, but contain comparisons to other submarine types. See Jeffrey Lewis, 'How capable is the 094?', Arms Control Wonk, 31 July 2007, http://lewis.armscontrolwonk.com/archive/1579/how-capable-is-the-094-23, and Jeffrey Lewis, 'China's Noisy New Boomer', Arms Control Wonk, 24 November 2009, http://lewis.armscontrolwonk.com/archive/2544/chinas-noisy-new-boomer.

34 The challenge of survivable communications is especially serious. For a review of Chinese open-source writing on this challenge, see Erickson and Goldstein, 'China's Future Nuclear Submarine Force: Insights from Chinese Writings'. Naval War College Review, vol. 60, no. 1, 2007, pp. 55–79.

35 A series of Pakistani missiles (including the Shaheen, Shaheen-2 and Ghaznavi) bear strong resemblance to missiles either deployed by China or seen at air shows in China. These missiles, however, may be partially modified – either by the Chinese for export or by Pakistanis themselves – making it difficult to say something definitive, such as Pakistani's Ghaznavi, sold as the M-11, corresponds to the missile known as the DF-11/CSS-7 Mod 1. The Shaheen-1, sold as the M-9, is usually thought to be a DF-15/CSS-6, although DF-15 variants look quite different from one another. The Shaheen-2 is said to be a missile called the M-18 seen at the Zhuhai Airshow in China in 1988.

36 Jeff Stein, 'CIA Helped Saudis in Secret Chinese Missile Deal', Newsweek, 29 January 2014, http://www.newsweek.com/exclusive-cia-helped-saudis-chinese-missile-deal-227283; Jeffrey Lewis, 'Why Did Saudi Arabia Buy Chinese Missiles?', Foreign Policy, 30 January 2014, http://www.foreignpolicy.com/articles/2014/01/30/why_did_saudi_arabia_buy_chinese_missiles.

37 'Annual Report to Congress: Military and Security Developments Involving the People's Republic of China 2009', Office of the Secretary of Defense, p. 66, http://www.defense.gov/pubs/pdfs/china_military_power_report_2009.pdf.

38 This is consistent with deployment numbers given in the 2009 Annual Report. See p. 48.

39 See, for example, 'Missile Commander Yang Yegong', CCTV, available at: http://www.cctv.com/news/special/C14394/

index.shtml; and 'Yang Yegong's analysis on our country's route of nuclear counterattack', https://web.archive.org/web/20051101235313/http://www.milnews.com/Article/wangyou/200508/4001.html.

40   I am indebted to Mark Stokes for highlighting the importance of grades in assessing where an officer stands in the protocol order.

41   *Directory of People's Republic of China Military Personalities*, 2013.

42   Mark Stokes, 'China's Nuclear Warhead Storage and Handling System', Project 2049 Institute, 12 March 2010, http://www.project2049.net/documents/chinas_nuclear_warhead_storage_and_handling_system.pdf.

43   It appears the launch battalion is the basic unit of firepower for the Second Artillery's nuclear force. See Ken Allen and Maryanne Kivlehan-Wise, 'Implementing PLA Second Artillery Doctrinal Reforms', in David Finkelstein and James C. Mulvenon (eds), *China's Revolution in Doctrinal Affairs* (2005).

44   'Ballistic and Cruise Missile Threat', United States National Air and Space Intelligence Center, 2013, http://www.fas.org/programs/ssp/nukes/nuclearweapons/NASIC2013_050813.pdf.

45   '2nd Artillery Soldiers hidden in underground caverns for 8 day exercise eat leeks and sweet peppers', Sina, 6 May 2013, http://mil.news.sina.com.cn/2013-05-06/0420723740.html.

46   On the challenges of life underground, see Mark Stokes and Ian Easton, 'Half Lives: A Preliminary Assessment of China's Nuclear Warhead Life Extension and Safety Program', Project 2049 Institute, 29 July 2013, pp. 13–15.

47   'Annual Report to Congress on the Military Power of the People's Republic of China 2013', p. 13.

48   'The People's Liberation Army Navy: A Modern Navy with Chinese Characteristics', Office of Naval Intelligence, https://www.fas.org/irp/agency/oni/pla-navy.pdf; 'China's Navy 2007', Office of Naval Intelligence, http://www.fas.org/irp/agency/oni/chinanavy2007.pdf; Ronald O'Rourke, 'China Naval Modernization: Implications for U.S. Naval Capabilities – Background and Issues for Congress', Congressional Research Service, 8 February 2012, http://www.hsdl.org/?view&did=701351.

49   In 1984, the US intelligence community was 'unable to identify the associated airfield storage sites' for the 'small number' of nuclear-capable aircraft that 'probably' had nuclear bombs assigned to them. The Defense Intelligence Agency (DIA) concluded that it was 'improbable that China's air forces have a strategic nuclear delivery mission' because 'it is unlikely that these obsolescent aircraft could successfully penetrate the sophisticated air defense networks of modern military powers'. Defense Estimative Brief: Nuclear Weapons Systems in China, pp. 3–4. In 1993, the US concluded that the 'Chinese Air Force has no units whose primary mission is to deliver China's small stockpile of nuclear bombs'. Report to Congress on Status of China, India and Pakistan Nuclear and Ballistic Missile Programs, http://fas.org/irp/threat/930728-wmd.htm.

50 'Guo Yafei, "Third Eye"', CNTV, 4 May 2011, http://military.cntv.cn/program/hpnd/20110504/105020.shtml.

51 'History: Second Artillery missile forces have become capable of strategic nuclear counterattack', Xinhua, 31 July 2005, http://news.xinhuanet.com/mil/2005-07/31/content_3282531.htm.

52 Stokes, 'China's Nuclear Warhead Storage and Handling System'.

CHAPTER FIVE

Strategic stability and regional security

The US has sought a dialogue on strategic stability with China since resuming military-to-military contacts in the mid-1990s.[1] At that time, the Clinton administration saw military-to-military contacts as part of a broader strategy of engaging China in a more cooperative relationship, a rationale that then-secretary of defense William Perry outlined in a now declassified memorandum to the service secretaries.[2]

Subsequently, the Clinton, Bush and Obama administrations each sought to initiate a dialogue with China on nuclear-weapons issues.[3] In April 2006, for example, President Bush and PRC president Hu Jintao committed to including nuclear issues in the bilateral dialogue.[4] Despite the agreement, then-secretary of defense Robert Gates complained on a visit to China that the PLA 'hadn't received the memo'.[5] Under the Bush Administration, the US and China eventually held a small number of meetings that included discussions of nuclear issues, notably a discussion at a session of the Defense Consultative Talks and an experts-level meeting in Washington.[6]

In the 2010 *Nuclear Posture Review*, the Obama administration committed to pursue a high-level bilateral dialogue on strategic stability with China. 'The purpose of a dialogue on strategic stability is to provide a venue and mechanism for each side to communicate its views about the other's strategies, policies and programmes on nuclear weapons and other strategic capabilities,' the authors of the *Nuclear Posture Review* wrote. 'The goal is to enhance confidence, improve transparency and reduce mistrust.' While such goals might seem anodyne, support for dialogue reflects a particular US experience with the Soviet Union and a sense that the mechanisms for US–China interactions are not commensurate with China's strategic importance and its military capabilities.

The US and China do discuss strategic and nuclear issues. In addition to one-off meetings, the two have a regular Strategic and Economic Dialogue, an undersecretary-level arms-control dialogue between the State Department and Department of Foreign Affairs, Defense Consultative Talks, as well as the opportunity for official meetings at side events, such as the Shangri-La Dialogue/Asian Security Summits organised by the IISS.[7] There are a number of so-called 'Track 2' non-governmental dialogues that often include participation by US officials. Yet, despite such meetings, most observers seem to feel that the depth and breadth of dialogue on nuclear issues are not yet equal to the stakes.

Pathologies in Sino-American dialogues

Despite the opportunities for official dialogue, the interactions themselves usually leave participants wanting. In particular, some have observed that existing dialogues – at either the official or non-government level – tend to make little progress. As one participant in the Track 2 process explained, 'I feel like we have a very good meeting, having built a foundation for a very important dialogue. When I step off the plane the next time, I feel like we build that same foundation again.'

One of the problems relates to no-first-use. As noted in Chapter One, Chinese officials have long sought a no-first-use pledge from the US, as a proxy for whether Washington will use, or threaten to use, nuclear weapons to coerce China. Meetings between the countries invariably include discussions of their respective views of no-first-use. For many Western strategists, no-first-use is not a credible commitment. There is no better exemplar of the Western view than the late Michael Quinlan, who eloquently rejected no-first use:

> If a nuclear-possessor country is desperate, whether it be nuclear weapons or something else that has made it so, it will not let its options be narrowed by a past promise made in peacetime tranquility and without reference to the calamities and iniquities which would have created the dire emergency. It might indeed decide that in all the circumstances (which could take many forms) it preferred defeat to the awful risks of embarking upon nuclear action; but the promise itself could not be conclusive, or even likely to weigh heavily, in that calculation. A nuclear possessor should certainly have a very strong preference, and may well have a very confident expectation, against ever needing to consider first use; but that is not what an NFU declaration would say – it would claim to express something more. To the extent that it seeks to guarantee that, it cannot be dependable.

Quinlan concludes by stating that 'we should have a deep distrust of taking up, on grounds of advantage in political presentation, positions that rest on false strategic premises'.[8]

Chinese officials and experts, on the other hand, have the opposite view. Chinese interlocutors have been educated in a context in which the strategic premises that Quinlan found false were asserted as Maoist orthodoxy. Moreover, few of these Chinese interlocuters are aware of the effect that the cynical Soviet no-first-use pledge has on Western experts, who regard no-first-use as a ploy to divide the US from its allies that Moscow would have violated on the first day of a general war in Europe.[9]

Instead, for Chinese officials and experts, no-first-use has served as a sort of proxy for whether the US would use nuclear weapons to coerce China into accepting unfavourable outcomes with regard to what Beijing sees as its vital interests, particularly relating to the status of Taiwan. Chinese interlocutors often directly press US officials for such a pledge, or ask Western academics why it's impossible. In some cases, Western interlocutors will provide detailed examples of the sort of dire emergency that could force Beijing to abandon its no-first-use pledge. For example, the US might use conventional weapons to threaten China's leadership or its strategic forces. To many Chinese, these hypothetical situations sound like a threat, rather than the sort of thought experiment common in Western academic settings. Americans will often, too, press the Chinese to be more transparent, something that strikes many Chinese as absurd, believing they have just been threatened. In many cases, these interactions can limit or even sabotage an otherwise productive meeting.

As a result, Chinese officials and experts continue to see a no-first-use pledge as a condition for meaningful engagement, while Americans continue to view such pledges as lacking credibility and harmful to the perception of US security commitments in Asia. The repetitive dysfunction – China's insistence the US make a no-first-use pledge and the refusal of the US to oblige – arises from a difference in strategic premises past which China and the US are unable to move .

Mutual vulnerability

If the US side finds no-first-use undesirable, it has been unable to offer China an alternative assurance that might entice Beijing to participate in a more productive dialogue. This is partly because Washington remains divided over the fundamental question of American nuclear strategy. There is no consensus within the US about whether it should make public pledges of what is now called 'mutual vulnerability' with China or other nuclear powers.

The term mutual vulnerability is an amalgam of two calumnies – 'mutual assured destruction' and 'assured vulnerability' – used by Donald Brennan, Herman Kahn and others to denigrate the Kennedy administration's strategy properly known as 'assured destruction'. As the US contemplated large deployments of strategic nuclear weapons in the early 1960s, the Kennedy administration, particularly then-secretary of defense Robert McNamara, sought a metric to cap the size of the strategic nuclear force. McNamara rejected minimum deterrence on the grounds that it abandoned any effort to limit the damage from a Soviet nuclear attack, while leaving allies exposed to nuclear coercion. McNamara's sizing construct involved a thought experiment, with the sequential use of a uniform force of 1mt bombs against the Soviet population and industrial targets. McNamara concluded that the damage inflicted on the Soviet Union would result in severely diminishing returns after 400 nuclear weapons, setting the size of the surviving force at 400 equivalent megatons.[10] McNamara named the strategy 'assured destruction' – the notion that once the US had a survivable force capable of assuring the destruction of the Soviet Union, additional nuclear weapons were unnecessary.

Even today, the frequent use of 'overwhelming' in official US documents to describe the damage that would be inflicted on a nuclear attacker signals a commitment to assured destruction as a measure of US capability, even if today's force-sizing constructs place a greater emphasis on the properties and capabilities of the nuclear force as a whole.

Herman Kahn and others argued against 'assured destruction' on the grounds that it did not constitute a sufficient commitment to a notion of prevailing in a nuclear conflict. Consequently, they derided the policy through name-calling – referring to it as either 'mutual assured destruction' or 'assured vulnerability'. During the 1970s many conservative critics accused the Nixon and especially Carter administrations of accepting US vulnerability and even Soviet superiority in nuclear forces.

In even elite discourse, however, the shared danger posed by nuclear weapons seemed to be an inescapable consequence of the nuclear age. The epithet 'mutual assured destruction' lost its potency as it became popularised as an accurate, if perverse, description of the arms race. Despite efforts under successive administrations to develop plausible scenarios for the use of nuclear weapons that fell short of national suicide, the zeitgeist embraced the futility of it all. Ronald Reagan, for example, was comfortable signing presidential guidance premised on the notion of prevailing in protracted nuclear war, while publicly and repeatedly expressing his sincere view that such a nuclear war could not be won.

The US political debate about whether to accept that the Soviet Union had an assured-destruction capability was never resolved. Rather, following the demise of the Soviet Union, the debate was bequeathed to China.

During this period in the 1990s, China completed its deployment of DF-5 and continued developing the solid-fueled DF-31 ICBM, steps toward what some scholars have called an 'assured retaliation' capability. US policymakers debated the same questions about China's strategic nuclear forces they had failed to resolve regarding the Soviet Union's. Should the US accept 'mutual vulnerability' with China? If so, what should the US say as a matter of policy? The shorthand for these questions became whether to treat China as a little Russia to be deterred, or as a big North Korea to be defended against.

Some George W. Bush administration officials, many of whom had long been critical of the notion of assured destruction in the Soviet context, were quick to deride the notion of 'mutual vulnerability' in the US–China strategic relationship. 'One [question] that is particularly important to address is this notion that we have a relationship of mutual assured destruction with China', then-undersecretary Douglas Feith testified to the Senate Committee on Foreign Relations. The US 'should not import into our thinking about China the cold war concepts of mutual assured destruction that applied between the United States and the Soviet Union', he stated.[11]

Others argued that 'mutual vulnerability' with China was not a choice but a fact that arose from China's ability to deploy survivable strategic forces. China's search for assured retaliation had succeeded. A Council on Foreign Relations Task Force, co-chaired by William Perry and Brent Scowcroft, concluded 'that mutual vulnerability with China – like mutual vulnerability with Russia – is not a policy choice to be embraced or rejected, but rather a strategic fact to be managed with priority on strategic stability'.[12]

As a practical matter, the US has long accepted the reality of its vulnerability vis-à-vis China, just as it accepted vulnerability with Moscow. Despite public statements from some officials during the Bush administration, as well as a somewhat misleading popular impression resulting from a partial leak of the 2002 *Nuclear Posture Review*, the Bush administration prioritised engagement with China and the importance of strategic stability.[13] By the end of the administration, the Secretary of State's

International Security Advisory Board (ISAB), chaired by former deputy secretary of defense Paul Wolfowitz, warned of China's 'creeping assured destruction capability' – and called on the Bush Administration to do more to arrest that vulnerability.

The incoming Obama administration, starting with the 2009 *Nuclear Posture Review*, also emphasised strategic stability with China and Russia – an implicit recognition of China's assured retaliatory capability. The president's nuclear-weapons employment guidance, signed in June 2013, formalised the decision to prioritise strategic stability with China along with Russia.

A second question emerges. If vulnerability is a fact of life, should the US recognise this fact publicly? The 2009 *Nuclear Posture Review*, as well as subsequent public statements, have stopped short on this point, even though the implicit recognition of vulnerability is evident. A new ISAB, by then chaired by William Perry, noted that 'Chinese leaders have been determined to maintain a credible nuclear deterrent regardless of US choices and will almost certainly have the necessary financial and technological resources to continue to do so'. It also concluded that vulnerability was a 'fact of life'. The report stopped short of providing language that might reassure China on this point, but called for a dialogue with China and allies 'on the role of nuclear weapons, and on the nature of US deterrent policy and capacity'.

Whereas the more recent ISAB report argued vulnerability did not prevent the US from credibly extending security guarantees to allies in the region, including Japan, others have cautioned that, even if vulnerability is unavoidable, recognising that would do little to reassure China, and would alarm allies. A Center for Strategic and International Studies (CSIS) task force, for example, was divided over the issue despite a consensus that extended deterrence could remain credible even in the face of vulnerability. Some members noted that recognising the underlying reality would have positive stabilising benefits on China's nuclear policies; others concluded from meetings in Tokyo that a formal recognition would unnerve US allies.[14] It is the question of allies, and their likely reaction, that plays the central role in this debate.

Regional security and US security guarantees

The nuclear relationship between the US and China includes US security guarantees to allies and partners in Asia, especially Japan and Taiwan. Extended deterrence – the notion that US security guarantees can deter aggression against allies and stabilise the region – significantly complicates otherwise simple models of balance and stability.

Policymakers in Washington, Tokyo and Taipei worry that the vulnerability of the US risks exposing allies to attack. In the NATO context, this concern was referred to as decoupling. French president Charles de Gaulle expressed the fundamental notion of decoupling when, in explaining when France needed an independent nuclear deterrent, he warned 'the Americans will never trade Washington for Paris'.

That concern resurfaced in the 1990s, when a Chinese official suggested that the US would never trade 'Los Angeles for Taipei'. This was immediately understood in the context of de Gaulle's remark.[15] This incident is often cited as evidence that Washington would not come to the aid of Taiwan for fear of an attack on Los Angeles. However, the American to whom the remark was made, Chas Freeman, later explained that the context was deterrence. The Chinese official said the US could not credibly threaten to use nuclear weapons to compel China to accept Taiwanese independence, since China could retaliate against an American nuclear attack. The Chinese interlocutor said:

> On three occasions before you threatened us with the use of nuclear weapons: once in the Korean War, twice in the Taiwan Straits crisis. You could do that then because we had no nuclear weapons. But now it is different. We have them also. If you hit our homeland, we will hit you. You care a lot more about Los Angeles than we do about Chinese cities.[16]

The reaction to this remark in Washington and allied capitals, whatever its original context, revealed a genuine concern that US vulnerability would undermine the credibility of US security guarantees to its Asian allies and partners. There may be broad consensus in Washington that vulnerability does not necessarily exclude the credible extension of deterrence, but most experts regard it as a significantly complicating factor that involves subjective factors of perception.

Sprint to parity

During the 2000s, a new concern appeared in Washington. Might China respond to further reductions in US strategic forces by 'sprinting to parity' – rapidly deploying large numbers of nuclear forces? Numerical parity is only a rough proxy for parity of capabilities, but given the emphasis on perception, many Japanese officials and experts have indicated that they would regard numerical parity as alarming. This concern initially grew out of China's large deployments of conventionally armed SRBMs, which appeared to some to be a harbinger of a future expansion of Chinese nuclear forces. The concern persisted into the Obama administration, with Secretary of Defense Robert Gates saying that 'reducing to very low levels of nuclear weapons – below 1,000 to 1,500 – offers the temptation to other powers to exceed those numbers and place us at a disadvantage, at a minimum in terms of perception'.[17]

The Bush administration sought to address this concern by articulating the notion of dissuasion – 'retaining a sufficient margin over countries with expanding nuclear arsenals to discourage their leaders from initiating a nuclear arms competition' – as a sizing criterion for nuclear forces. Officials argued that the deployed force needed to be a factor of three, or better yet four, larger than China's stockpile of nuclear weapons available for deployment on ballistic missiles.

There is little historical evidence to suggest Chinese leaders have placed an emphasis on numerical parity. To reach parity with the United States at foreseeable levels, China would probably need to expand its capacity to produce fissile material, particularly plutonium. This would require the construction of new reactors, something that is possible but would require several years.[18]

At the same time, China has dramatically expanded its conventional missile arsenal over the past decade, and is now adding conventionally armed medium- and intermediate-range ballistic missiles, alongside cruise missiles. More than a decade has passed since the onset of China's conventional missile deployments without a corresponding increase in nuclear arms. With the benefit of hindsight, the sudden expansion of conventionally armed SRBMs represented a shift in emphasis by the Second Artillery rather than a harbinger of a nuclear arms race.[19] US policymakers remain reluctant to build down to parity with China, but there is less concern within the Obama administration that China might build up to the levels provided for under the New START agreement or those proposed as the basis for a follow-on agreement.

On the other hand, the sprint-to-parity scenario has given way to a concern in Tokyo that strategic stability might enable Chinese conventional aggression. Over the past decade, China has become more assertive regarding maritime territorial claims, alarming Japan which maintains administrative control over the Senkaku Islands that China claims as its own Diaoyu Islands. Many policymakers in Tokyo have concluded that China's growing assertiveness reflects its growing military capabilities. Few believe nuclear weapons would deter Chinese maritime incursions. But, there is growing concern about the so-called stability–instability paradox, in which stable strategic deterrence enables limited conventional aggression. China's heavy investment in conventionally armed ballistic and cruise missiles is usually described in US documents as presenting an anti-access/area-denial (A2AD) threat that supports more aggressive efforts to pursue Chinese claims along its periphery.

Following consultations with Japanese officials and experts, the authors of the 2009 *Nuclear Posture Review* emphasised the goal of strengthening 'regional security architectures' in order to convey that efforts to engage China on strategic stability would not come at the expense of regional security. The issue remains a serious concern for US allies. Any sustainable dialogue involving strategic stability must consider the need to provide credible security guarantees to regional allies and partners.

Alert operations

There remains the possibility that a regional crisis between the US and China, either involving the status of Taiwan or control over disputed maritime territories, could escalate to a wider war that implicates each country's nuclear forces. Although a nuclear exchange would seem grossly disproportionate to the material stakes in any foreseeable crisis, such a crisis may involve broad principles involved that touch on the core interests of each nation. The series of crises that led Europe into the First World War, as well as the Cold War moments of danger involving Soviet missiles in Cuba and the status of Berlin, illustrate how a small crisis can be a fulcrum on which larger forces can lever nations into war.

In such a case, Chinese military textbooks and other documents express a consistent view that the US is likely to use the threat of nuclear weapons to attempt to compel China to accept an unfavourable resolution. Chinese historical accounts emphasise US 'nuclear blackmail', and concerns about possible US coercion often appear in contemporary dialogues with Chinese officials and scholars. This viewpoint is expressed so consistently that it would be surprising if Chinese leaders interpreted US nuclear signals in another fashion.

For their part, US officials often express concern that China's nuclear forces are intended to deter American involvement, invoking the fear of decoupling that worried de Gaulle. Just as China's conventional forces appear intended to prevent US intervention, many Americans worry that China's nuclear forces may deter the US from coming to the aid of an ally or partner. There is a robust debate, for example, about the feasibility of a US defence concept called Air–Sea Battle. Critics charge that Air–Sea Battle – a modification of a Cold War concept for Air–Land Battle – would entail strikes on the Chinese mainland. Such strikes may run an unacceptable risk of nuclear escalation. Proponents suggest that escalation can be addressed by either measures to contain conventional conflict or more sophisticated counterforce capabilities and missile defences to deter escalation.

If, in the midst of a crisis, the US signalled its will to resist Chinese nuclear threats, much as Washington did with Pyongyang by including nuclear-capable bombers in military exercises during a tense period, Beijing is likely to interpret the signal as coercion rather than a deterrent threat. In such a case, Chinese military texts and other documents suggest that one option is to alert the Second Artillery in order to demonstrate China's ability and willingness to retaliate against a nuclear aggressor with nuclear weapons.[20] It seems very likely, however, that just as the Chinese leadership would have interpreted a US signal as a threat, a US president would conclude that Chinese missiles being sent into the field and submarines flushed to sea represent a prelude to an attack.

As seen in Chapter One, textbooks are easy to misinterpret, especially when the descriptions of conventional and nuclear operations are so different. Readers have misread references to 'lowering the nuclear threshold' to mean that China intends to use nuclear weapons early in conflict, rather than as a strategy of last resort to prevent or stop conventional attacks on strategic assets. The history of US alert operations suggests such operations have inherent escalatory potential. Scholarly studies of past US strategic alerts reveal that orders are frequently misunderstood and ambiguous events misinterpreted to confirm the sense of crisis.[21]

Chinese forces, too, offer considerable opportunity for confusion, as well as reasons for concern. China deploys conventional variants of the nuclear-armed DF-21. It is also developing a conventionally-armed anti-ship variant of the missile. Such ambiguities would colour the US interpretation of a Chinese decision to place strategic forces on alert. Chinese leaders may believe they are sending a signal of resolve; a US president might conclude that these are preparations for an attack. Moreover, the Chinese have invested in a number of capabilities that add pressure on the US to escalate a conflict, including anti-satellite weapons that might allow China to disrupt communications, navigation and missile warning.

This situation is likely to worsen as both the US and China invest in longer-range conventional strike systems. A major rationale for conventional prompt global strike in the US includes targets in central China such as anti-satellite locations. Yet the development of such systems only increases China's incentive to target space assets, while further blurring the line between nuclear and conventional forces. The nuclear forces of both sides are becoming increasingly entangled with one another as conventional forces become more capable. The result is less clarity and time in a conventional crisis that takes on a nuclear character.

The recent history of crisis management should be alarming. The US and China have experienced several tense crises in recent years, arising from the operation of military forces in close proximity to one another. In 2001, a US EP-3E reconnaissance aircraft collided with a Chinese fighter jet, killing the Chinese pilot and forcing the EP-3E to land on Hainan. China detained the crew for 11 days, while the two countries negotiated the return of the crew and the aircraft. In March 2009, the US Navy announced that 'five Chinese vessels shadowed and aggressively maneuvered close to the USNS Impeccable in the South China Sea…'. It was operating within the boundaries of international law, yet the Chinese viewed the ship as conducting surveillance for anti-submarine warfare activities. Chinese and US anti-submarine activities that would look different if the Chinese submarines were nuclear-armed and deploying to sea in crisis. These two incidents represent early warnings of the continuing potential for incidents that could escalate between the two powers.

Conclusion

Successive US administrations have attempted to improve the dialogue on national security issues with China since the nadir of 4 June 1989. Progress toward this goal has been fitful and marked by setbacks. Despite a handful of official interactions and a second track of dialogue among non-governmental experts, Beijing and Washington have not succeeded in creating a true bilateral dialogue about nuclear forces, policies and posture. The prospects for arms-control negotiations in a bilateral context are nil.

One reason the United States and China have struggled to create a progressive dialogue on nuclear-weapons issues that builds on successive meetings relates to differing views on no-first-use pledges. China continues to adhere to a no-first-use pledge issued in 1964. Chinese diplomats have pressed the US to issue its own pledge since that time, viewing no-first-use as a proxy for whether Washington will use, or threaten to use, nuclear weapons to coerce China. The US has consistently refused to do so because American officials almost uniformly regard such a pledge as lacking credibility and complicating its security guarantees to Asian states. Moreover, US officials and experts regard China's policy as not credible. Chinese officials, however, show little interest in revisiting their views about how Beijing talks about nuclear weapons, even as China develops nuclear forces and operational concepts that complicate such a simple pledge. This debate is fraught with the potential for misapprehension. When Western interlocutors provide detailed examples of the sort of dire emergency that could force Beijing to abandon its no-first-use pledge, their Chinese counterparts often perceive that they are being threatened.

The prospects for dialogue are further complicated by the unresolved debate in US circles over nuclear strategy, particularly the vexing question of whether the US should accept privately and acknowledge publicly that other nuclear powers such as China have an assured capability to inflict unacceptable damage on the United States. Although as a practical matter, virtually all US policymakers accept the vulnerability of the United States to China's nuclear forces, Americans remain locked in a fierce political debate over whether this is a reality that must be accepted and acknowledged or a choice that can be rejected.

Public acceptance by the US of mutual vulnerability, which would go some way to meeting China's concerns encapsulated in calls for a no-first-use pledge, would also raise questions by many US allies including Japan about the credibility of the security guarantees that the US has provided. The acceptance of vulnerability does not necessarily render such commitments incredible, but it does significantly complicate the picture.

The US position is further complicated by a concern that, as it reduces its nuclear force, China may be tempted to 'sprint to parity' by building up its own nuclear arsenal to the point of numerical parity with the United States. China's large deployments of conventionally armed SRBMs initially appeared to many a harbinger of a future expansion of Chinese nuclear forces. With time, however, it seems the sudden expansion of the Second Artillery's short- and medium-range missile forces reflected an interest in boosting its conventional capabilities rather than engaging in a nuclear arms race with the US. While few American officials worry about China building to parity in nuclear forces today, many remain wary of reductions that may bring the United States far closer to China's level.

Finally, in the US and across Asia, many officials and experts remain concerned about the US-Chinese strategic balance. This is partly a matter of the stability–instability paradox – the notion that a stable strategic relationship could permit one side to engage in conventional aggression. Given the growing militarisation of maritime disputes in the South and East China seas, it is understandable that there is concern that strategic stability might make Asia safe for conventional warfare.

Despite these challenges, the two parties face a compelling case for emphasising strategic stability. A political crisis involving Taiwan or Japan that involves military forces could easily escalate in a manner that implicates each country's nuclear forces. In such a crisis, Chinese leaders fear the US will use the threat of nuclear weapons to attempt to compel them to accept an unfavourable outcome – and believe Chinese nuclear weapons may blunt a coercive threat. US leaders, conversely, fear that China's nuclear forces are intended to deter the US from coming to the aid of its allies. If, in the midst of a crisis, the US took steps to signal its will to resist Chinese nuclear threats, China's leaders might interpret those steps as an effort to coerce Beijing rather than to deter it. For its part, it is possible that China – expecting to be the subject of nuclear coercion – would then signal its resolve to resist such pressure by putting its own nuclear forces on alert. Would the US recognise this as a signal of resolve, or preparations for an attack?

These problems are likely to become more pressing as both the US and China invest in advanced conventional capabilities including missile defences, anti-satellite weapons and, most importantly, long-range conventional strike systems. The nuclear forces of both sides are becoming increasingly entangled with one another as conventional forces become more capable and, to some extent, more strategic in character. The result is less clarity and time in a conventional crisis that escalates to nuclear threats and beyond.

Notes

[1] Kurt Campbell and Richard Weitz, 'The Limits of U.S.-China Military Cooperation: Lessons from 1995–1999', *Washington Quarterly,* vol. 29, Winter 2005, pp. 169–86.

[2] William J. Perry, Memorandum for the Secretaries of the Army, Navy, and Air Force, 'U.S.–China Military Relationship', August 1994. Reprinted in 'China and the United States: From Hostility to Engagement', 1960-1998, National Security Archive Electronic Briefing Book No. 19, Jeffrey T. Richelson (ed.), 24 September 1999, http://www2.gwu.edu/~nsarchiv/NSAEBB/NSAEBB19/12-01.htm.

[3] Campbell and Weitz, 'The Limits of U.S.–China Military Cooperation'.

[4] Other steps during the Bush administration include then-Secretary of Defense Rumsfeld's visit to the PLA Second Artillery headquarters in 2005; House Armed Services Committee Chairman Ike Skelton's August 2007 visit to

the Academy of Military Sciences that included a meeting with then-Second Artillery commander Jing Zhiyuan; the December 2007 Defense Consultative Talks (DCTs) between General Ma Xiaotian and then-Under Secretary of Defense for Policy Eric Edelman; the April 2008 US–China Nuclear Dialogue between General Huang Xing and Brian Green; and a June 2008 US–China Security Dialogue between Assistant Foreign Minister He Yafei and then-Acting Under Secretary for Arms Control and International Security John Rood. Summaries of most of these meetings are available in the leaked State Department cables. For a list of military-to-military contacts, including defence department engagement on nuclear issues with China, see Shirley A. Kan, 'U.S.–China Military Contacts: Issues for Congress', Congressional Research Service, 12 June 2014, https://www.fas.org/sgp/crs/natsec/RL32496.pdf.

5   Describing his November 2007 trip to Beijing, Gates writes that 'Bush and Hu had agreed in April 2006 to pursue bilateral discussions of nuclear strategy, but it was pretty plain that the People's Liberation Army hadn't received the memo'. Robert Gates, *Duty: Memoirs of a Secretary at War* (New York: Knopf, 2014), p. 195. The US and China ultimately included a 'discussion of nuclear policy at the December 2007 Defense Consultative Talks (DCTs) between General Ma Xiaotian and Under Secretary of Defense for Policy Eric Edelman'. This meeting is described in a leaked 2 February 2011 cable from the US Embassy in Bejing titled 'U.S.–China Security Dialogue Working Lunch: Strategic Security, Missile Defense, Space, Nonpro, Iran'. The document is available at: http://www.telegraph.co.uk/news/wikileaks-files/china-wikileaks/8299322/U.S.-CHINA-SECURITY-DIALOGUE-WORKING-LUNCH-STRATEGIC-SECURITY-MISSILE-DEFENSE-SPACE-NONPRO-IRAN.html.

6   For an unusually detailed description of the April 2009 meeting, see Bonnie Glaser, 'Chock-full of Dialogue: SED, Human Rights, and Security', *Comparative Connections*, July 2008, http://csis.org/files/media/csis/pubs/0802qus_china.pdf.

7   Secretary Gates notes that he found the Shangri-La Dialogue 'a good opportunity to do a lot of bilateral business', noting that he was able to use a 2010 speech to engage with Chinese officials after Beijing withdrew an invitation to protest arms sales to China. Gates, *Duty*, p. 145.

8   Michael Quinlan, *Thinking About Nuclear Weapons: Principles, Problems, Prospects* (New York: Oxford University Press, 2009), p. 101.

9   On differing Chinese and American views of no-first-use, see Gregory Kulacki and Jeffrey Lewis, 'No First Use in Sino-American Dialogue: Dilemma and Solution', *Foreign Affairs Review*, vol. 29, no. 5, May 2012.

10   This was a thought experiment. The US had neither a force of uniform 1mt bombs nor target cities as such.

11   Administration's Missile Defense Program and the ABM Treaty,

Hearing before the Committee on Foreign Relations, United States Senate, 24 July 2001.

12   William J. Perry, Brent Scowcroft and Charles D. Ferguson, 'US Nuclear Weapons Policy', Independent Task Force Report No. 62, Council on Foreign Relations, 2009, p. 4, http://www.cfr.org/proliferation/uzsz-nuclear-weapons-policy/p19226.

13   The 2002 *Nuclear Posture Review*, leaked portions of which identified a conflict with China as an 'immediate contingency' that helped determine the US number of nuclear weapons on day-to-day alert, was conflated with the *National Security Strategy* and its emphasis on pre-emption, creating a public impression of bellicosity that officials would struggle to counteract during Bush's term in office.

14   'Nuclear Weapons and U.S.–China Relations: A Way Forward', CSIS, March 2013, pp. 19–20, http://csis.org/files/publication/130307_Colby_USChinaNuclear_Web.pdf.

15   De Gaulle's remark is often quoted but seldom cited, with any number of cities involved in the hypothetical exchange: Chicago for Lyon, New York for Paris, Hamburg or Bonn. It may be that de Gaulle was fond of making the comparison. He certainly made it at least twice during the 1961 Berlin Crisis, once directly to President Kennedy and again to members of Congress. See Document 30, 'President's Visit, Memorandum of Conversation (US/MC/1), Paris, 31 May 1961', in *Foreign Relations of the United States, 1961–1963*, Volume XIV, 'Berlin Crisis, 1961–1962', and Memorandum of Conversation with the President and the Congressional Leadership, 6 June [Briefing on President Kennedy's European Trip], Memorandum of Conversation, 7 June 1961', p. 1.

16   Milton Leitenberg, 'Memorandum of Conversation with Charles Freeman', Jr., 9 October 1996 (unpublished account).

17   Gates, *Duty*, p. 408.

18   Construction of commercial power reactors, for example, usually takes about 50 months from first concrete to fuel loading. Additional time would be required to modify a design for plutonium production, as well as the time necessary to produce and separate the plutonium. On commercial construction timelines, see 'Nuclear Power in China', World Nuclear Association, April 2014, http://www.world-nuclear.org/info/Country-Profiles/Countries-A-F/China--Nuclear-Power/.

19   It is worth noting that were China to undertake a sprint to parity for the purpose of undermining the credibility of US security guarantees in Asia, it would have to do so publicly to achieve the desired effect. I am indebted to Werner Merkwürdigliebe for this point.

20   For example, one exercise is described in Dong Jushan and Wu Xudong, 'Build New China's Shield of Peace', *Beijing Zhongguo Qingnian Bao*, 1 July 2001.

21   Scott D. Sagan, 'Nuclear Alerts and Crisis Management', *International Security*, vol. 9, no. 4, Spring 1985, p. 136.

China's initial acquisition of nuclear weapons and ballistic missiles was driven by a desire to possess the same 'sophisticated weapons' as other major powers. From the very beginning, in the late 1950s, the Chinese leadership was committed to developing large, multimegatonne thermonuclear warheads that could be delivered at intercontinental ranges by ballistic missiles. This was an audacious goal for the poor, technologically inept China of the Great Leap Forward era.

Nevertheless, China moved quickly in its nuclear testing programme to develop thermonuclear warheads, burning thermonuclear fuel in its third nuclear test (prior to demonstrating a missile-deliverable fission device) and successfully conducting a staged thermonuclear explosion with its sixth test. At the same time, China pursued an ambitious missile-development programme called Eight Years, Four Missiles (*Banian Sidan*) based on technological steps toward an ICBM.[1]

Despite relatively rapid advances in research and development, China was slow to deploy operational forces, completing its deployment of first-generation nuclear-armed ICBMs in 1988. China's emphasis on technological goals, rather than near-term acquisition of usable weapons systems, reflected the unique circumstances that led to China's acquisition of nuclear weapons. Chinese leaders initially expected substantial Soviet assistance in developing nuclear weapons. After the Soviets suspended assistance in 1960 and amid the lingering chaos of the Great Leap Forward, the Chinese leadership split over the issue of strategic programmes. Afterward, support for the development of sophisticated weapons would depend on the broader theme of China's economic development and emphasised the possession of advanced capabilities, rather than their battlefield uses.

This approach underpinned China's unusual force structure. The dominance of the research and development community meant relatively little emphasis was placed on acquiring large numbers of missiles or nuclear weapons. Moreover, the prioritising of technological acquisition meant that new systems were developed with comparatively little emphasis on operational concepts. The PLA itself was hardly in a position to do more than accept systems developed by the defence community.

Since the 1990s, however, the PLA has become a dominant factor in defense policy. China folded the institutional remnants of what has been called China's techno-nationalist elite into the newly created General Armaments Department of the PLA. The PLA, including the Second Artillery, is far more professional than it was in the past and has received significant spending increases since the mid-1990s. What is more, China is rapidly acquiring and integrating major technological developments including solid-fueled ballistic missiles and advanced information technologies.

With a new leadership in China it's worthwhile to ask how China's changing technological, political and security situation will shape its strategic forces. These changes raise interesting questions for China's operationally deployed force of approximately 100–200 nuclear warheads. The US intelligence community expects this number to grow, though not significantly. China is currently modernising its missile force, introducing new solid-fueled missiles to replace or complement the first generation of missiles deployed between 1966–1996. China has followed the liquid-fueled DF-3, DF-4 and DF-5 missiles with the solid-fueled DF-21, DF-31 and DF-31A missiles.[2]

In recent years, the Second Artillery has deployed large numbers of conventionally-armed SRBMs and cruise missiles, and placed comparatively more emphasis on conventional missile operations. Today over half of China's launchers and brigades are assigned conventional, not nuclear-armed, missiles. China appears to keep conventional and nuclear units at separate bases, albeit this judgment is difficult to make with any degree of certainty and questions exist about the deployment of conventional and nuclear-armed DF-21 ballistic missiles.

At the same time, China's navy is finally ready to deploy nuclear-armed ballistic–missile submarines. China has at least four *Jin*-class ballistic missile submarines, each with 16 launch tubes for the new JL-2 submarine-launched ballistic missile.[3] Significant questions remain as to how China will operate its fleet of SSBNs. It is possible that, rather than maintaining a continuous at-sea deterrent, China will patrol episodically, flushing submarines to sea in a crisis.

Why did China build such a small nuclear force? Why does it exacerbate the inherent vulnerability of such a force by keeping warheads separate and maintaining a retaliatory-only doctrine? One reason is bureaucratic. Advocates for nuclear weapons in China's defence hierarchy were initially located with the research and development community. The bureau-cracy responsible for defence production, on the other hand, advocated spending scarce funds on production of tanks, ships and aircraft.

The first generation of Chinese leaders also had specific, Maoist ideas about the role of weapons. Chinese Communist leaders first used the term 'paper tiger' to refer to reactionaries, not nuclear weapons, in 1946. The reference is a metaphorical allusion to 'an older Maoist revolutionary maxim which holds that men and politics, rather than weapons and economic power, are the determining factors in war'.[4] In context, referring to nuclear weapons as paper tigers merely indicates that the balance of nuclear weapons is not likely to be decisive in conflict, and that the technical details matter very little.

As a result, the formal process of developing plausible operational concepts for the Second Artillery did not begin until the early 1980s. Over the years, the Second Artillery has struggled to create such concepts within the strictures of no-first-use. In recent years, Chinese military experts appear to have become especially concerned with precision strikes against strategic forces or other high-value targets.

These differences pose an interesting challenge. If Chinese leaders believe that nuclear weapons are intended to defeat attempts at coercion, and Chinese textbooks suggest China might signal its resolve in a crisis by nuclear forces on alert or announcing it would not be bound by its no-first-use pledge, would US policymakers understand the signal? Or would they interpret Chinese signals as escalatory, further deepening a crisis?

US officials do not believe US threats to use nuclear weapons are coercive, but defensive. Moreover, they are reluctant to acknowledge the viability of China's deterrent, worrying that a public recognition would alarm US allies, particularly Japan. These views, however, exacerbate the Chinese sense that, in a crisis, further steps would be necessary to induce caution in Washington.

These, then, are the pieces of the puzzle: Future military crises, given the evolution of US and Chinese nuclear and conventional forces, may prove highly escalatory. Yet, taking steps to enhance stability at the strategic level might worsen the already deteriorating conventional environment. For many years Americans and Chinese have sought to discuss these issues, but official and non-governmental efforts have produced little difference in policy or mutural understanding.

Engaging China in a formal process of arms control does not seem likely. The Chinese have expressed no interest in joining the bilateral arms-control process between the US and Russia, a process that was unhealthy even before Moscow's annexation of Crimea and invasion of eastern Ukraine, as well as reports that Moscow was violating the 1987 Intermediate-Range Nuclear Forces Treaty. The official view in Beijing is that Russia and the US must make further reductions before China will discuss its much less numerous nuclear forces.

There are many asymmetries between the three forces that preclude a trilateral arms-control process in the foreseeable future. Finally, while China has participated in multilateral arms-control negotiations, the Conference on Disarmament in Geneva remains moribund and unable to bring negotiations on a Fissile Material Cut-off Treaty.

How might the US and China move past current disputes over no-first-use and transparency to resolve crisis stability questions without sacrificing regional security? The experience with Taiwan offers a useful precedent. It is worth recalling that in 1972, the US and China crafted the Shanghai Communiqué in a way that worked around the seemingly insurmountable barrier that Washington did not even recognise Beijing as the rightful government of China. The artfully worded document did not obscure the parties' differences, but rather made clear both shared many other interests. Even if Washington and Beijing could not agree on the status of Taiwan, they could agree that there was only one China and that the status of Taiwan was to be decided by the Chinese themselves. That was enough.

A similar agreement is needed on the subject of nuclear weapons and strategic stability. It likely centres around two pledges: the US must offer a security assurance that makes clear it does not seek to negate China's deterrent, even if China must accept that the assurance will not take the form of a no-first-use pledge; for its part, China must make clear that it does not seek numerical parity with the US or to otherwise undermine US security guarantees in the region. Such an agreement – a Shanghai Communiqué for strategic stability – would offer a number of advantages. First, it would move beyond formulaic calls for no-first-use and transparency, which crowd out meaningful dialogue between the US and China. It would open dialogue on many questions that remain unresolved. US and Chinese policymakers are likely to continue to disagree about China's modernisation of its strategic forces, as well as the US development of missile-defence and conventional strike capabilities. The mutual statements in a formal communiqué create an opportunity for both parties to explore how these modernisation programmes can reinforce, rather than undermine, the status quo.

Second, an agreement would make possible a set of limited transparency measures. Chinese objections to transparency tend to emphasise that US demands are open-ended. If the US and China were to agree to the pledges suggested above, however, they might also agree to tailored transparency measures intended to build confidence in specific commitments. For example, if China pledged not to seek numerical parity, it might disclose information about the number of Second Artillery bases and brigades, even if not the precise number of

launch units per brigade. The US, in turn, might provide brief-
ings on the actual capabilities of planned missile-defence and
conventional strike programmes.

Third, dialogue on strategic stability may enable other progress in other areas, such as multilateral arms control. Such a
dialogue may help resolve Chinese concerns about a fissile-
material cut-off treaty, persuading Beijing to end its policy of
enabling Pakistan's obstruction of the treaty in the Conference
on Disarmament. Similarly, dialogue with the US may
improve chances of the two countries ratifying the 1996 CTBT.
Opponents of the test ban in Washington might see the benefit
of keeping China's nuclear-test data to the 45 explosive tests it
conducted through 1996, particularly if the two parties are able
to explore confidence-building measures related to subcritical
testing and other activities at their test sites.

Fourth, dialogue may provide important benefits for stability in the event of a crisis. Currently, China keeps its strategic
forces off alert, with warheads stored separately from missiles.
In the event of a crisis, Chinese policymakers may intend to
alert these forces to signal their resolve. It remains unclear if
a US president would understand such a signal, or interpret
Chinese mobilisation as preparation for a launch. In peacetime,
it is merely cumbersome that the two countries have radically
different ideas about the role of nuclear weapons and a limited
ability to communicate with each other. In a crisis, it could be
downright dangerous.

Such an agreement would not resolve all of the challenges
facing the strategic relationship, but it would provide a frame-
work by which these challenges are managed. At the onset
of China's nuclear programme in the 1950s, the two parties
viewed one another with hostility, each suspecting the other
of plotting the use of force – including the use or threat of use
of nuclear weapons – to change the status quo. In large part,

these underlying fears remain unchanged despite the dramatic evolution in their relationship over the past 60-plus years. Even if nuclear weapons are a 'paper tiger', they retain the capacity to frighten us. Whether that fear is enough to compel us to respond to the shared danger they pose remains to be seen.

Notes

[1] Lewis and Xue, *China Builds the Bomb*, pp. 211-212.

[2] China appears to be developing additional missiles, including another MRBM (identified as the CSS-X-11) and possibly a new ICBM (sometimes called the DF-41).

[3] China constructed a single *Xia*-class ballistic-missile submarine in the 1980s, but this submarine does not appear to have ever become operational.

[4] Ralph L. Powell, 'Great Powers and Atomic Bombs Are "Paper Tigers"', *China Quarterly*, no. 23, July–September 1965, pp. 55–63.

INDEX

Adelphi books are published eight times a year by Routledge Journals, an imprint of Taylor & Francis, 4 Park Square, Milton Park, Abingdon, Oxfordshire OX14 4RN, UK.

A subscription to the institution print edition, ISSN 1944-5571, includes free access for any number of concurrent users across a local area network to the online edition, ISSN 1944-558X. Taylor & Francis has a flexible approach to subscriptions enabling us to match individual libraries' requirements. This journal is available via a traditional institutional subscription (either print with free online access, or online-only at a discount) or as part of the Strategic, Defence and Security Studies subject package or Strategic, Defence and Security Studies full text package. For more information on our sales packages please visit www.tandfonline.com/librarians_pricinginfo_journals.

2015 Annual Adelphi Subscription Rates

Institution	£615	$1,079 USD	€910
Individual	£217	$371 USD	€296
Online only	£538	$944 USD	€796

Dollar rates apply to subscribers outside Europe. Euro rates apply to all subscribers in Europe except the UK and the Republic of Ireland where the pound sterling price applies. All subscriptions are payable in advance and all rates include postage. Journals are sent by air to the USA, Canada, Mexico, India, Japan and Australasia. Subscriptions are entered on an annual basis, i.e. January to December. Payment may be made by sterling cheque, dollar cheque, international money order, National Giro, or credit card (Amex, Visa, Mastercard).

For a complete and up-to-date guide to Taylor & Francis journals and books publishing programmes, and details of advertising in our journals, visit our website: http://www.tandfonline.com.

Ordering information:
USA/Canada: Taylor & Francis Inc., Journals Department, 325 Chestnut Street, 8th Floor, Philadelphia, PA 19106, USA. **UK/Europe/Rest of World:** Routledge Journals, T&F Customer Services, T&F Informa UK Ltd., Sheepen Place, Colchester, Essex, CO3 3LP, UK.

Advertising enquiries to:
USA/Canada: The Advertising Manager, Taylor & Francis Inc., 325 Chestnut Street, 8th Floor, Philadelphia, PA 19106, USA. Tel: +1 (800) 354 1420. Fax: +1 (215) 625 2940. **UK/Europe/Rest of World**: The Advertising Manager, Routledge Journals, Taylor & Francis, 4 Park Square, Milton Park, Abingdon, Oxfordshire OX14 4RN, UK. Tel: +44 (0) 20 7017 6000. Fax: +44 (0) 20 7017 6336.

The print edition of this journal is printed on ANSI conforming acid-free paper by Bell & Bain, Glasgow, UK.